Acting-In
2nd Edition

Adam Blatner, M.D., is the Director of Pediatric Consultation—Liaison Services at the Bingham Child Guidance Clinic and an assistant professor of child psychiatry at the University of Louisville School of Medicine, both in Louisville, Kentucky. He is also a board-certified trainer of psychodrama. He received his B.A. from the University of California at Berkeley in 1959 and his M.D. from the University of California Medical Center in San Francisco. His specialty training included an adult and child psychiatric residency at the Stanford University Medical Center in Palo Alto, CA, and at the Cedars-Sinai Medical Center in Los Angeles. Dr. Blatner was in the U.S. Air Force at its regional hospital in England as the medical director of its child psychiatry service. On returning to California in 1972, he began private practice in the San Francisco Bay area. Prior to his present position, he was on the staff of the Menninger Foundation in Topeka, Kansas. He is the author of several books and articles on the subject of psychodrama and its applications.

ACTING-IN

Practical Applications of Psychodramatic Methods
Second Edition

Adam Blatner, M.D.

SPRINGER PUBLISHING COMPANY
New York

To David and Alisa, my son and daughter,
whose natural childhood play
helped me understand Moreno's
insights regarding
spontaneity and creativity.

Copyright © 1988 by Springer Publishing Company, Inc.

Springer Publishing Company, Inc.
536 Broadway
New York, NY 10012

93 94 95 96 / 7 6 5 4

LIBRARY OF CONGRESS
Library of Congress Cataloging-in-Publication Data

Blatner, Adam.
    Acting-in : practical applications of psychodramatic methods /
Adam Blatner.—2nd ed.
        p.   cm.
    Bibliography: p.
    Includes index.
    ISBN 0-8261-1401-6
    1. Psychodrama.   I. Title.
    [DNLM: 1. Psychodrama.   WM 430.5.P8 B644a]
    RC489.P7B47 1989
    616.89'1523—dc19
    DNLM/DLC
    for Library of Congress   88-19960
                                                                    CIP

Printed in the United States of America

Contents

Foreword to the First Edition

In 1921, I created psychodrama out of the earlier work I did with group psychotherapy, sociometry, and improvisatory theatre. Since then I have written numerous books and scores of articles on the subject. Dr. Blatner's book, *Acting-In*, will be a good adjunct to my writings. This is an excellent work on the subject.

I am especially pleased that Dr. Blatner notes the theological basis of the method of psychodrama.

I have always tried to show that my approach was meant as much more than a psychotherapeutic method—my ideas have emphasized that *creativity* and *spontaneity* affect the very roots of *vitality* and spiritual development, and thus affect our involvements in every sphere of our lives. Furthermore, I have always wanted to have people attend to the processes of health, as well as to the problems of illness; thus I am glad Dr. Blatner has noted the applications of psychodrama in the home, school, and world of business.

When I first met Dr. Blatner in 1968, he was a resident in psychiatry at Stanford University. At that time he showed me a collection of writings by others in the field of psychodrama, along with a few additions of his own—a syllabus he had assembled entitled "Practical Aspects of Psychodrama." I encouraged him to continue his interest in psychodrama and to do more of his own writing. Apparently, he has taken my advice.

I am further pleased with the different audiences to whom this book can be addressed: for those who are interested in learning about psychodrama, it can be an introduction; for those who are practitioners, these materials can comprise a useful handbook; and for the serious student, *Acting-In* is an up-to-date and extensive resource for references and background materials.

I wish the author every success in this undertaking.

J. L. MORENO, M.D.

Preface to the First Edition

The ancient Greeks used the drama as a ritual for the purpose of evoking a group catharsis. While the other artistic media have also served to express feelings and images, it was the drama that fully utilized the collective element in the service of objectifying the cross-currents of the soul and the dilemmas of the human condition. The drama in this sense had healing powers in that it clarified the unexpressed experiences and helped the individual to accept more fully the various facets of the personality.

The synthesis of the media of drama with the insights of modern psychology was chiefly developed by J. L. Moreno, M.D., in his work with psychodrama. The various applications of psychodramatic methods have been found to be effective in the fields of modern psychotherapy and education.

The major purpose of this book is to introduce the reader to the fundamental elements and basic principles related to the use of psychodramatic methods. Along with practical suggestions regarding technique, I include discussions of some of the theoretical bases of the use of the method. It is expected that the reader may need to modify these approaches to meet the requirements of specific situations, and such creative adaptations are to be encouraged. To facilitate the reader's commitment to a serious study of the method, I also include references at the end of each chapter.

The reader may find many potential applications of the psychodramatic method, such as: in the fields of mental health, in group and individual psychotherapy, therapeutic community and drug abuse programs, occupational and activity therapy, and so forth; in the fields of education, from the preschool level to the postgraduate professional training programs; in the churches, in pastoral counseling and group meetings; in business and industry, for organizational development and leadership or personal relations training; and various other kinds of experiential workshops.

In all of the above-mentioned fields, the use of action-oriented psychodramatic methods can complement traditional verbal approaches in order to facilitate the development of personal awareness and interpersonal sensitivity. It is the hope of the author that this book may help to increase the responsible applications of psychodramatic methods.

A. B.
Palo Alto, California
May, 1973

Preface to the Second Edition

Since the first edition of this book was published in 1973, changes have occurred that warrant an updating in this second edition. J. L. Moreno died in 1974, and the American Society for Group Psychotherapy and Psychodrama went on to become a more democratically controlled professional association, taking over the editing of the *Journal of Group Psychotherapy, Psychodrama, and Sociometry,* establishing the American Board of Examiners in Psychodrama, Sociometry, and Group Psychotherapy to certify practitioners and trainers, and in other ways continuing to bring the field to a level of professionalism on a par with other subspecialties of psychotherapy.

This book has become one of the major textbooks in the field in the last 15 years, serving a growing international audience, including England, Australia, Europe, and South America. It has been translated into Dutch, Japanese, Swedish, and Spanish. For those who noticed that the first edition was written by Howard Blatner, it is necessary to note that I changed my name in 1978 to Adam Blatner, and the stimulus for it is an anecdote worth sharing. This name change was occasioned by a workshop led by Zerka Moreno, who used as a warm-up an invitation to consider how we felt about our names and whether we would choose a different one. In my second marriage and renewed life, I felt free to seriously explore my wife's suggestion and exchange a first name I had never liked for one I preferred. It took a few months, and finally one came.

In the previous edition of *Acting-In*, I listed various training institutes, but many changes have occurred in the ensuing years: many addresses are no longer correct, some of the directors have died, new institutes have been created, and it has become better to have a single clearinghouse for this information. From the 1940s through the 1970s, Moreno's original institute, the World Center for Psychodrama in Beacon, New York, helped serve that function. However, in the early 1980s, the institute was closed, part of the property was sold, and the original psychodrama stage was moved to the Jonathan Steiner Hall at Boughton Place in Highland, New York.

Most of the practical elements outlining the method remain the same in this edition because over the years I have received consistent verification that they present the approach in a clear fashion. The references have been expanded to reflect a more current status, with less significant ones being deleted. However, the chapters on training and history have required significant revision because of the many changes in the field.

Recently, I wrote a companion to *Acting-In*, titled *Foundations of Psychodrama: History, Theory, and Practice*, also published by Springer Publishing Company (1988). A good deal of theory is explicated there, along with a compendium of psychodramatic techniques. Most importantly, I tried to communicate a sense of the underlying philosophy, the spirit of psychodrama. This more fundamental attitude is what makes the application of psychodramatic methods something that can be integrated into many aspects of life, as well as the mainstream of psychotherapy.

My interest in adapting psychodramatic methods to applications beyond the clinical setting, to include new ways of facilitating education, management, family relations, recreation, and so forth, has continued to develop. Another book my wife Allee and I wrote recently applies the psychodramatic method to the more general activity of cultivating imagination and spontaneity in make-believe play. This is aimed especially at adults, although it can be adapted for use in teaching creative dramatics or for helping parents to play with their children. *The Art of Play* (Blatner & Blatner, 1988) represents a natural outgrowth of the possibilities for applying psychodrama in broader areas of human endeavor.

Finally, I want to express my deepest appreciation to my wife, Allee, for the extensive help she has given me in the revision of this book.

ADAM BLATNER, M.D.
Louisville, Kentucky
February, 1988

REFERENCE

Blatner, A., & Blatner, A. (1988). *The art of play: An adult's guide to reclaiming imagination and spontaneity.* New York: Human Sciences Press.

Introduction

Many of the most powerful active approaches in contemporary psychotherapy and education are derived from the
method of psychodrama, in which a person is helped to *enact*
the problem instead of just talking about it. The purpose of
this book is to introduce some practical applications of the
psychodramatic method to readers from a variety of disciplines.

The psychodramatic method integrates the modes of cognitive analysis with the dimensions of *experiential* and *participatory involvement*. It not only partakes of the advantages of
group therapy, but its uses of physical movement also bring
the component of nonverbal cues to the attention of the
participant. This is especially important not only for those
who have little capacity for intellectual and verbal exploration (e.g., children, psychotics, delinquents, etc.), but also
for those who tend to overintellectualize their experiences.
The most significant advantage of psychodrama, however, is
that it converts the participant's urge toward "acting-out"
into the constructive channel of "acting-in," which leads to
insight.

Acting-out refers to the psychological defense mechanism
by which an individual discharges internal impulses through
symbolic or actual enactment (Kellerman, 1984; Ormont,
1969). Since the rationale for this defense mechanism occurs

1

largely outside of consciousness, the individual experiences no sense of mastery or growth of self-understanding through the behavior. If the drive toward action could be channeled, the person might be able to make better use of the feelings. Through psychodramatic enactment, the impulses and their associated fantasies, memories, and projections are made consciously *explicit*, which serves to express these feelings while simultaneously developing the individual's self-awareness (Fingarette, 1969).

In the use of the psychodramatic method, the tendency toward acting out is encouraged, but within a structured group experience (Schwartz & Schwartz, 1971). What emerges is an enactment that turns the impulses into insights. Thus psychodrama facilitates not acting-out, but what should be called "acting-in": the applications of *action* methods to the exploration of the psychological aspects of human experience (Bromberg, 1958; Zeligs, 1957).

In addition to the task of clarifying emotional conflicts, the psychodramatic method can be applied to the challenge of developing human potentialities. Through "acting-in," the individual can be reintroduced to many dimensions of personal experience that have been neglected in our contemporary, overintellectualized society: creativity, spontaneity, drama, humor, playfulness, ritual dance, body movement, physical contact, fantasy, music, nonverbal communication, and a widened role repertoire. Western civilization has relegated many of these pursuits to childhood, the theater, or mythology, and in so doing has drained our souls of their richest treasures. It is essential that we learn to recognize the vitality that can only grow within the context of play, and to cultivate and refine play so that we can preserve the spirit of childhood in our adult lives (Blatner & Blatner, 1988). Indeed, the task of integrating the experiential worlds of feelings, sensation, and imagination into our existences may become a major goal of contemporary education and psychotherapy. In this book I will attempt to explicate in some detail how the psychodramatic method can reinforce this sense of play and experience.

PSYCHODRAMA AND PSYCHOTHERAPY: A HISTORICAL COMPARISON

Psychodrama and psychoanalysis need not be at odds; rather, they are similar in that they act as *root* methods. Psychodrama, like psychoanalysis, can serve as a source of theory, technique, and as a method of research. Furthermore, both approaches have been modified extensively and have been incorporated into other methods.

My own view is to liken psychodrama to the woodwind instruments of the orchestra: their introduction vastly extended and deepened the range of effects that were possible. This is because the mixture of two methods (or what Marshall McLuhan would call "media") results in the development of a totally new form that is more powerful and qualitatively different from the result of simple additive effects. So, too, does the addition of psychodramatic methods to conventional verbal forms extend the power of psychotherapy. Verbal and nonverbal forms need not be at opposite poles, for it is quite possible to interweave the aspects of cognitive and experiential, objective and subjective, and other polarities of human experience (Blatner, 1968).

Psychoanalysis marked the beginning move toward the integration of the nonrational. The Western world, involved in the Industrial Revolution and the romanticization of the "scientific" and the "objective," associated the realms of nonobjective reality with all that was regressive, primitive, infantile, and foolish (Roszak, 1969). However, psychoanalysis itself attempted to fit the "scientific objective" context in order to obtain respectability. (Carl Jung's "mystical" ideas caused a major split in the early psychoanalytic movement, but, like psychodrama, they have become increasingly recognized as being relevant to the needs of our contemporary culture.)

During the second half of the twentieth century, the technological-philosophical pendulum has begun to swing back again toward an incorporation of the dimensions of emotion, sensation, and imagination into the world of personal experience. The excesses and oversaturation of technological and objective consciousness are being recognized. For example, the concept of psychotherapy is no longer being restricted to the modes of dyadic or group verbal discussion. A "new eclecticism" that includes action in psychotherapy is being increasingly accepted (Abroms, 1969). Moreover, changes in the field of psychotherapy, the phenomena of encounter groups, improvisation in theater and music, and innovations in education exemplify the trend toward the experiential mode of involvement.

The importance of these phenomena was foretold in the first quarter of the twentieth century by Jacob L. Moreno, a Viennese psychiatrist who developed the methods of sociometry and psychodrama, as well as being a major contributor to the evolution of group psychotherapy. In an effort to reintroduce the spirit of growth-through-play into our lives, he emphasized ideas about spontaneity, creativity, action, self-disclosure, and risk-taking in "encounter," importance of the present (he coined the term "here-and-now"), the significance of touch and nonverbal communication, the cultivation of imagination and intuition, and the value of humor and the depth of drama. The psychodramatic method and its derivatives are the primary vehicles by which people can learn to develop these potentialities in themselves.

CAUTIONS

At this point, I wish to note some cautions for the reader. Psychodrama is no panacea: any romanticizing of a single approach is dangerous, as it blinds one to the limits of that approach and the values of other methods. Psychodramatic techniques can be very powerful, and it behooves the practitioner to develop skills with humility and commitment. The therapist or group leader must be helped to build a broad range of skills and a depth of ability with which to apply them, for mere technique is not enough. With creativity and sensitivity, the practitioner must learn to know and work with the psychological dimensions of a client's life.

I would strongly encourage the reader to obtain some supervised training in the use of psychodrama before attempting to apply any but the most elementary methods. The mastery of psychodrama itself requires a significantly greater degree of training than can be described in any one book. One cannot learn these approaches through "cookbook" reading, any more than one can learn art or music. Nevertheless, I hope that the reader may be stimulated to use some of the methods and to continue to explore the theories and applications of an eclectic approach to psychotherapy and education. I further emphasize the importance of supplemental readings from the bibliography at the end of this book.

In summary, therefore, I am presenting this book as an introduction to the theory and practice of using the psychodramatic method in a wide variety of psychotherapeutic and educational settings. I believe that the applications of these methods can do much to facilitate the reintroduction of the elements of spontaneity and creative empathy into human experience.

REFERENCES

Abroms, G. (1969). The new eclecticism. *Archives of General Psychiatry, 20,* 514–523.

Blatner, A. & Blatner, A. (1988). *The art of play: An adult's guide to reclaiming imagination and spontaneity.* New York: Human Sciences Press.

Blatner, H. A. (1968). Comments on some commonly held reservations about psychodrama. *Group Psychotherapy, 21* (1), 20–25.

Bromberg, W. (1958). Acting and acting out. *American Journal of Psychotherapy, 12,* 264–268.

Clements, C. C. (1968). Acting out vs acting through: An interview with Frederick Perls, *Voices.*

Fingarette, H. (1969). Self deception. In R. F. Holland (Ed.), *Studies in philosophical psychology.* New York: Humanities Press.

Kellerman, P. F. (1984). Acting out in psychodrama and in psychoanalytic group therapy. *Group Analysis, 17*(3), 195–203.

Kreitler, H. & Eblinger, S. H. (1961). Psychiatric and cultural aspects of the opposition to psychodrama. *Group Psychotherapy, 14,* 215–220.

Ormont, L. R. (October 1969). Acting-in and the therapeutic contract in group psychoanalysis. *International Journal of Group Psychotherapy, 19,* 420–432.

Roszak, T. (1969). *The making of a counter-culture.* New York: Doubleday.

Schwartz, L. & Schwartz, R. (1971). Therapeutic acting-out. *Psychotherapy: Theory, Research and Practice, 8*(3), 205–207.

Zeligs, M. A. (1957). Acting-in. *Journal of American Psychoanalytic Association, 5,* 685–706.

1

The Basic Elements of Psychodrama

Psychodrama is the method by which individuals can be helped to explore the psychological dimensions of their problems through the *enactment* of conflict situations, rather than by talking about them. The methods derived from psychodrama can be applied and modified in a wide variety of settings. Although psychodrama and its related methods have much in common with the dynamics of psychotherapy and group-centered education, the terminology in this book will relate to the essentially *dramaturgical* nature of the process.* Some of the more common terms are listed below.

The *protagonist* is the person who is the subject of the psychodramatic enactment. Whether acting as a client, patient, student, trainee, group member, or other form of participant, when a person portrays a personal life situation he/she is the protagonist (Moreno, 1971).

The *director* is the person who guides the protagonist in the use of the psychodramatic method in order to help the pro-

---

*Note: Often, uninformed journalists erroneously describe a play, movie, or piece of literature that has psychological dimensions as a "psychodrama." Actually, psychodrama is a process wherein the participants explore more healthy alternative solutions to their real problems. The display in the media involves characters playing roles melodramatically, usually tragically, and without the role of the director as healing guide.

tagonist explore a problem. The director may be the person in the group who is ordinarily considered to be the group leader, therapist, teacher, or counselor.

The *auxiliary ego*, or simply the *auxiliary*, is the term for anyone besides the protagonist and the director who takes part in a psychodrama. Usually the auxiliary ego portrays someone in the protagonist's life, such as a wife, employer, or "another part" of the protagonist. One of the special roles and techniques that can be played by the auxiliary is the *double;* this is discussed further in Chapters 2 and 3.

The *audience* refers to the others present during the psychodrama. The audience may be the psychotherapy group, a seminar or class in school, or other members of the protagonist's family. Unlike a conventional audience, the audience in psychodrama often takes an active role in participating in the protagonist's exploration of feelings.

THE VEHICLES OF PSYCHODRAMA

The *stage* is the area in which the enactment takes place. The stage may be a formal platform for psychodrama; it may be the area in the middle of a group; or the actual locus of the conflict *in situ* (e.g., the reenactment and exploration of a conflict between children on the playground where it was occurring earlier). There are some props and structures, however, that can make the dramatic function even more effective.

In the original form of psychodrama, a stage such as that shown in Figure 1 was used. The three levels, lighting arrangements, balcony, and design were all empirically developed to facilitate the power of the enactments. Any of these components can be useful if included (Enneis, 1952). Other designs have been created such as having part of the

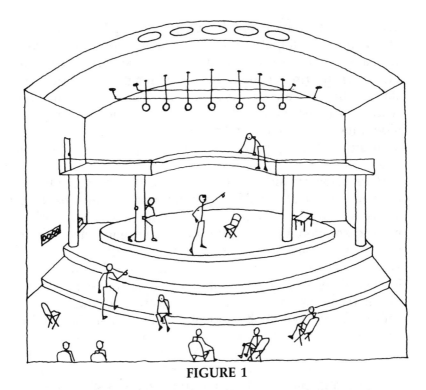

FIGURE 1

stage sunken, as was done at the St. Louis State Hospital (Moreno, 1971, p. 497).

The main stage should be at least 12–15 feet in diameter. A raised platform that can easily be stepped onto is helpful in subliminally establishing the "as-if" set in the participant. (The Greeks used the term "proscenium arch" to mark the border of the stage—when one crosses the "arch" he enters or exits from the "world" of the drama.) As a protagonist and auxiliary ego moves toward the stage, their stepping upward indicates to all concerned that they are entering the "psychodramatic reality."

On the stage there may be a few props: Some lightweight chairs and a simple table are most often used. Pillows, a mattress, and a variety of other props can also be useful. The *chair* is not only for sitting on, but, when empty, can "hold" any fantasied or projected figure. It can also become a barricade, a platform, or an indicator of height, authority, or status. The *table* can become a building-top, a desk, a judge's seat, a breakfast-room table, or a cave in which to cringe or hide. Pillows and foam rubber bats can be used for fighting, pounding, beating, protection, or perhaps to be held as a baby.

More elaborate aids are not essential but can provide remarkable effects. Special lighting, for example, may be used to evoke many moods: red to represent hell, a bistro, or an intense emotional scene; blue for death scenes, heaven, or the sea; total blackness for isolation, loneliness, or a need to enact something privately; and dim light for dream scenes. Music, either skilled accompaniment or emotionally meaningful recorded songs, can be a powerful adjunct to psychodrama as well. Body movement is also facilitated by rhythmical forms of music (Fine, 1962).

MAJOR FORMS OF PSYCHODRAMATIC ENACTMENT

Psychodrama refers to an enactment involving emotional problem solving in terms of *one person's* conflict; it is "protagonist-centered." The drama may shift among the many facets of the protagonist's life—his past, present, and future. Usually psychodrama moves toward relatively deep emotional issues (Kellerman, 1987; Kipper, 1988). Psychodrama as a form of psychotherapy was originated around 1920 by J. L. Moreno, M.D., who then went on to develop many modifications that would be appropriate for a variety of group situations.

Sociodrama is a form of psychodramatic enactment that aims at clarifying *group* themes rather than focusing on the individual's problems. Although a person may participate as a protagonist in a sociodrama, the focus of the group task is on the problems of the *role* played in the drama rather than on a personal life situation. Thus, sociodrama could be termed *group-centered*.

A group of nurses in training, for example, might use sociodrama to explore the challenge of dealing with certain kinds of patients. When one of the nurses (as the protagonist) becomes involved in a scene, the emotional issues of the problem will be expressed. However, the director should bring out those facets of the relationship that would likely be present in many or *most* nurse–patient interactions; those feelings unique to the protagonist would *not* be emphasized. In other words, it would be inappropriate in a sociodrama for a director to deal with the *personal* aspects of the nurse who is the protagonist, for this might imply to the others in the group that the difficulties in the interaction were due to deficiencies unique to that nurse (Kelly & Philbin, 1968).

A sociodrama can function as a *warm-up* for a protagonist-centered psychodrama in settings where exploration of the individual's life is part of the group task. Sociodrama, however, is sufficient in itself as a modality for exploring the stresses involved in the relationships between police and citizen, parent and child, boy and girl, customer and salesman, different races, employer and employee, or student and teacher.

Role-playing, like sociodrama, is a derivative of psychodrama. Although some people use all these terms interchangeably, most professionals would consider role-playing to be more superficial and problem-oriented. Expression of deep feelings is not usually part of most role-playing operations. Rather, the goal of role-playing tends to be working out alternative and more effective approaches to a general problem. Industry, school, and professional training contexts are more likely to utilize this modality in meeting tasks such as developing interviewing skills, dealing with difficult children, handling customer relations, and so forth.

Psychodramatic techniques, used in a variety of contexts, are also known by terms such as *action methods, encounter techniques, growth games, theater games, structured experiences,* or *nonverbal exercises.* Although many of these techniques were originated by Moreno and other psychodramatists, many ideas have also been modified from the fields of guided fantasy, psychosynthesis, sensory awakening, Gestalt therapy, Bioenergetics, improvisatory dramatics, and other related methods. Whatever their origin, psychodramatic techniques can be applied in many situations where formal psychodrama, sociodrama, or role-playing might not be appropriate. Indeed, one of the chief aims of this book is to encourage the reader to begin to experiment with the use of psychodramatic methods first, and then to practice the more complex approaches.

THE TECHNIQUES OF PSYCHODRAMA

Scores of psychodramatic techniques exist, along with hundreds of variations and modifications. Most of the major techniques are described in different sections of this book. These techniques can be used in order to accomplish a variety of goals.

In order to *clarify a protagonist's feelings,* the techniques of *the double, soliloquy, multiple selves,* and *monodrama* are used.

For heightening and facilitating the *expression of emotion,* the director may use *amplification, asides,* and the exaggerations of nonverbal communications, along with exaggerations of the dimensions of height, space, and position.

The protagonist may be aided in becoming aware of personal behavior *(self-confrontation)* through the use of techniques such as *videotape playback, role reversal, behind-your-back, audience feedback, chorus,* and *nonverbal interaction exercises.*

Goals and values may be clarified through the use of the *magic shop* or the *future-projection techniques.*

Support can be given with the techniques of *ego-building, sharing,* and the judicious use of *physical contact,* such as hugging or holding.

Issues of *group process* can be clarified through the techniques of the *spectrogram* and *sociometry.*

Finally, there are many special techniques that can be used along with psychodrama, such as *hypnosis* and *guided fantasy.*

Through the use of the above-mentioned techniques, the director can help the protagonist to enact a broad range of experiences: scenes from everyday life, as well as dreams, memories, delusions, fears, and fantasies.

AN OUTLINED DESCRIPTION OF A TYPICAL PSYCHODRAMATIC ENACTMENT

I. The Warm-up (see Chapter 4)
   A. The director warms herself up.
   B. The group discusses goals, roles, fees, limits, time arrangements, and so forth.
   C. Getting acquainted; exercises are used that introduce group members to each other.
   D. The director leads the group in action exercises that build group cohesion and spontaneity.
   E. This often leads to a discussion of what the participant experienced in the warm-up exercises, which in turn leads to the emergence of a theme of common interest to the group, or to an individual's problem.
   F. One of the group members is selected to be the pro-

tagonist, who will enact his own or the group's problem.

II. The Action (see Chapter 5)

    A. The director brings the protagonist to the stage, where the problem is briefly discussed (Schramski, 1979).

    B. The conflict is redefined in terms of a concrete example—one that could be *enacted*.

    C. The director helps the protagonist to describe the setting in which a specific action occurs, thus "setting the stage."

    D. The protagonist is instructed to play the scene as if it were occurring in the "here-and-now."

    E. The director brings other members of the group forward to take the parts of other significant figures in the protagonist's drama—these people then become the *auxiliary egos*.

    F. The opening scene is portrayed.

    G. The director helps the auxiliary egos to learn their roles by having the protagonist change parts with them (reverse roles) for a brief period during which the protagonist then portrays the behavior of the other figures in his drama. As the auxiliaries learn their roles, the protagonist gives them feedback until he feels that the scene is being enacted in an essentially similar way to the way he pictures it in his mind. This "molding" activity furthers the warm-up of the auxiliary egos and the protagonist himself.

    H. The scene continues with the director introducing other psychodramatic techniques that function to elaborate on the feelings being expressed (e.g., soliloquy, the double technique, asides, etc.).

    I. As the enactment unfolds, the director uses a variety of other techniques in order to explore different facets of the protagonist's experience.

1. Ambivalence is explicitly demonstrated through the use of several individuals (auxiliaries) on the stage, each portraying a different part of the protagonist's psyche.
2. Empathetic or projected feelings of the protagonist can be enacted through role reversal.
3. Self-confrontation for the protagonist may be utilized through the *mirror technique.*
4. Significant past memories are reenacted.
5. Future plans, hopes, and fears can be symbolically realized and explored.
6. The protagonist's suppressed emotions—guilts, resentments, fears, yearning—can all be expressed using a variety of facilitating techniques.

J. The action may be carried to a point where the protagonist experiences a sense of having symbolically enacted those behaviors that had been suppressed—fulfillment of *act hunger.*

K. The protagonist is helped to develop other adaptive attitudinal and behavioral responses to his situation—this is called *working through* (see Chapter 6). (In role-playing contexts, this process may become the predominant task of the group.) Some specific techniques used in working through include:

1. Repeat role-playing of the conflict, with the protagonist trying a different approach with each attempt.
2. Modeling by other group members, to show how *they* would deal with the problem.
3. Role reversal between the protagonist and his auxiliary egos—the other figures in his enactment—so that the protagonist can discover, through actually *experiencing* the other person's situation, some clues as to what behaviors might achieve the desired effect.

III. Closure (see Chapter 6)
  A. Following the main action, the director helps the protagonist to receive some supportive feedback from the other group members. Rather than encouraging an intellectualized analysis of the protagonist's problem, the director encourages the group members to *share* with the protagonist the feelings they had related to the enactment.
  B. The director may proceed to use a variety of supportive psychodramatic techniques.
  C. Further discussion by the group ensues.
  D. Finally, the director either goes on to the process of warming-up to another psychodramatic enactment with a different protagonist, or moves toward terminating the group, possibly using a variety of *closing techniques.*

REFERENCES

Enneis, J. M. (1952). Establishing a psychodrama program. *Group Psychotherapy, 5*(3), 111–119.

Fine, R. (1962). Psychodance. *Group Psychotherapy, 15*(3–4), 203–206.

Kellerman, P. F. (1987). A proposed definition of psychodrama. *Journal of Group Psychotherapy, Psychodrama & Sociometry, 40*(2), 76–80.

Kelly, H. S. & Philbin, M. K. (1968). Sociodrama: An action-oriented laboratory for teaching interpersonal relationship skills. *Perspectives in Psychiatric Care, 6*(3), 110–115.

Kipper, D. A. (1988). On the definition of psychodrama: Another view. *Journal of Group Psychotherapy, Psychodrama & Sociometry, 40*(4), 164–168.

Moreno, J. L. Psychodrama. (1971). In H. I. Kaplan & B. J. Sadock (Eds.), *Comprehensive group psychotherapy,* (Chapter 9). Baltimore: Williams & Wilkins.

Schramski, T. G. (1979). A systematic model of psychodrama. *Group Psychotherapy, Psychodrama & Sociometry, 32,* 20–30.

2

The Auxiliary Ego

The auxiliary ego, sometimes simply called the auxiliary, is the term used for any person other than the director who participates in a psychodramatic enactment in order to help the protagonist explore his problem. Auxiliary egos play a variety of roles not only in psychodramatic, sociodramatic, and role-playing situations, but they also can be used as an action technique in ongoing psychotherapy or development groups (Zinger, 1975).

TYPES OF AUXILIARY EGO ROLES

The role of a significant other person, someone in the protagonist's *social atom**, for example, a wife, son, employer, friend, therapist, and so forth. When this person is the main character in the enactment playing opposite the protagonist, he is occasionally called *the antagonist.*

The double, the auxiliary who takes the role of the protagonist's *alter ego.* In this role, the auxiliary ego as double helps the protagonist to express his inner feelings more clearly. The technique of using an auxiliary in the role of

---

**Social atom:* Moreno's term for the complex of all the significant figures, real and fantasied, past and present, who relate to a person's psychological experience.

double is extremely important in psychodrama and will be discussed more fully in the next chapter.

The part of someone more distant, in a general role—a policeman, teacher, client—but no specific person personally known to the protagonist (this is more commonly used in sociodrama and has a rather peripheral role in a psychodrama).

The role of a fantasied figure, for example, God, a judge, a tempter, an idealized father the protagonist never knew, the "Prince Charming" who will rescue the protagonist.

An inanimate object to which the protagonist relates, for example, his bed, doorway, house, the desk that mocks its owner (the protagonist) for his lack of self-discipline: "Hey! What about all this work you've piled on me? You're always saying you'll get to me, but you never do!"

An example of this would be that of a woman who, exploring her relationship with her daughter-in-law, acts the part of her daughter's-in-law living room. "It" becomes embarrassed when the mother-in-law pays a visit, and says in an aside to the audience: "Oh-oh, here she comes . . . she's going to want to change everything!" Then, to the mother-in-law: "Don't you think I can possibly look good unless you have a hand in fixing me up?"

The role of an abstract concept or a collective stereotype, for example, "they," "society," "contemporary youth," "the church," "justice," and so forth.

FUNCTIONS OF THE AUXILIARY EGO

The auxiliary ego helps the protagonist to explore his situation by acting toward him in the role assigned: the employer who behaves in a "calling-on-the-carpet" manner, the mother who worries or infantilizes, the spouse who argues but doesn't listen.

The performance of this role must be similar in essence to the behavior of the person being represented, but need not be exact. Indeed, a small amount of unexpected behavior on the part of the auxiliary ego often increases the protagonist's spontaneous involvement in coping with that challenge.

The auxiliary ego's behavior evokes a similar response: if the auxiliary whispers, the protagonist tends to respond as if there were a secret; if the auxiliary "escalates" into screaming and cursing, this may bring out a similar expressiveness on the protagonist's part. (This is called a "symmetric" response.)

The auxiliary ego's role may stimulate the protagonist to take a "complementary" role: if the auxiliary acts judgmental, the protagonist responds with defensiveness, rebelliousness, or gives an explanation; if the auxiliary acts helpless, the protagonist becomes protective. In the same way, dominance provokes submissiveness, etc.

The auxiliary ego's speaking in the "here-and-now" and his manner of encountering "in-role" tends to pull the protagonist into the interaction as if it were actually happening there for the first time. Thus the auxiliary functions to involve the protagonist more deeply in the psychodramatic enactment, which in turn tends to bring out his basic conflicts and suppressed feelings more rapidly and completely.

There are times, however, when the protagonist ought to play all the parts in the enactment himself. The drama with no auxiliary egos is called *autodrama* or *monodrama*. The protagonist may shift places using one or two empty chairs, and have an encounter between different parts of himself, or with his projection of someone with whom he has a conflict. Fritz Perls used monodrama as a core technique in Gestalt therapy.

Some of the indications for the directors choosing to use monodrama instead of using auxiliary egos include:

when the protagonist is in individual therapy

when the director wants the protagonist to find out that the "answers" to his questions are to be found within himself

when the protagonist could play both roles in an encounter much more easily than could any auxiliary ego

THE SELECTION OF THE AUXILIARY EGO

The role of the auxiliary ego is usually played either by one of the group members or by a *professional auxiliary ego*. The professional or trained auxiliary is most often found in situations where there is an ongoing program of psychodrama. The person may be a psychodrama director-in-training, a nurse on an inpatient ward, a co-therapist, or simply another staff member who is experienced in the use of psychodramatic methods.

The main advantage of using a professional auxiliary ego to play key roles is that he is experienced in warming himself up to the roles involved. An auxiliary who can play a variety of roles and easily express feelings (i.e., one who has a high degree of spontaneity) can galvanize a psychodramatic enactment. Furthermore, a great deal of spontaneity is especially necessary in roles that involve the exhibition of grossly crude, childish, cruel, arrogant, "bitchy," seductive, or humiliating behavior.

On the other hand, even when there are trained auxiliary egos present, there are times when it is best to allow different group members to be auxiliaries and play the various parts. For example, in a psychodrama in which a girl is exploring her competitive feelings toward other women, the auxiliary ego who is to be the man over whom the girls fight may be played by one of the shy men in the group. While his role as auxiliary serves a function in the girl's exploration of her problem, it may also benefit him. Even in warm-up techniques, group members may be picked to play parts that would normally oppose their habitual style: the constricted, "nice-guy" type might benefit by acting in the role of a "villain"; the shy, plain girl may discover some sexy aspects of herself by playing a "seductress"; a "stuffed shirt" may loosen up by playing a role which gives him permission to be silly, that is, a child, a monster, or an animal.

Another factor to be considered in the selection of auxiliary egos is the degree to which a group member identifies with the protagonist's situation, or with the position of one of the other parts in the enactment. If an auxiliary ego has a conflict in his own life that is similar to that of the protagonist, the value the psychodrama has for the protagonist can either be increased or decreased. To some extent, the "carry-over" from the auxiliary's own situation can validly be applied to the protagonist's life, but beyond that it can become a disconcerting pressure that only confuses the protagonist. Unless the director is alert to the auxiliary ego's behavior and applies firm control, the auxiliary can impose artificial issues upon the protagonist's drama. The director may occasionally check with the protagonist by asking: "Is this the way your wife, mother, etc., acts?"

TECHNIQUES IN THE SELECTION OF THE AUXILIARY EGO

Most often the director asks the protagonist to choose the auxiliary for specific roles. It may be useful to later ask the protagonist to examine the determinants for his "intuitive" choice.

The professional *auxiliary*, often a staff member or experienced group member, is chosen by the director.

The director may choose a group member to be an auxiliary because she believes either that the auxiliary would benefit, that the auxiliary could play the role well, that the auxiliary has familiarity with the role, or that the role is so narrowly defined that there would be only one person in the group who could either play or identify with that role.

The director may ask for suggestions from the group as to which member should take each role.

The director may ask for volunteers, for any who are empathetic and have a desire to play a specific auxiliary role: "Has anyone here been in Joe's situation and could 'double' with him?"

After an enactment the auxiliary is often asked not only to "share" his own feelings regarding the protagonist's situation, but is also invited to comment on his own experiences "in-role" as an auxiliary ego. As an example, in an enactment a woman was playing a scene with her perfectionistic father and herself as an eight-year-old child. The man chosen to be the auxiliary playing the father had to yell at the protagonist-as-child. Afterwards, during the sharing, this man, then in his forties and a rather mild-mannered person, said he was also raised by a harsh, judgmental father. On being asked how he felt playing the role, he replied that he found it difficult. It brought back many memories, but he wished he could feel more often the power associated with giving himself permission to express aggression openly.

Another technique is for the director to ask the group members after an enactment to discuss roles in which they would be most or least comfortable. The group could also discuss which roles would be most helpful for each to play in the future. These discussions further help the group members to develop receptivity toward playing the auxiliary ego role in later enactments.

OTHER AUXILIARY EGO ROLES

The auxiliary chair. An empty chair can be used in a warm-up (see Chapter 4, p. 53) and can also represent the significant other in an enactment. If the protagonist feels angry, he may beat the chair with cushions or kick the chair—actions he would not be permitted to perform with a "live" auxiliary ego. The chair can also be a barrier to get around, representing either an emotional or physical block. Lastly, two empty chairs are often used as props for the protagonist to move to and from. For example, the director says: "Joe, in this chair, the nice, obedient part of you speaks to your mother (played by an auxiliary); in that chair, the rebellious, sullen part of you can also talk to your mother in a way you have never expressed yourself" (see Figure 2).

The silent auxiliary ego. There are times when it is sufficient to keep an auxiliary ego on stage even if he is to be silent, for he can provide support simply by being present.

THE AUDIENCE AUXILIARY EGO

Members of the audience can be asked to give comments, either in the discussion period or during a break in the enactment. Sometimes specific roles will be assigned: someone to "observe" the process; someone to "identify with" the protagonist and/or one of the auxiliary's roles; someone to try to think of alternate solutions.

Several group members may chant or repeat some fixed statement in the background as a chorus, such as the contents of a hallucination, obsession, delusion, judgment attitude, secret wish, and so on.

The audience may be used as objects of the protagonist's statements: The protagonist makes a statement reflecting an

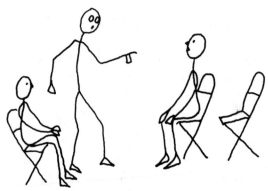

FIGURE 2

internalized attitude, the director may have that attitude "played out" until it becomes hollow, for example, the protagonist says, "I am an adult," but continues to act childishly. The director says, "Go around to each person in the group and tell him/her that."

Using behind-the-back technique. The protagonist may benefit from "overhearing" what others say about him. The director has the protagonist turn his back, and announces that he is "no longer present." The group then discusses the protagonist as if he were not in the room (Corsini, 1954).

Audience members can double for each other and speak out on issues where they might otherwise be silent. A trained auxiliary ego might start this, and the others follow. For example, the audience is getting bored, but says nothing. An audience double exaggerates the group's slouching, nonverbal behavior and shouts, "Boy, is this boring!" or "He's manipulating the heck out of us!"

GUIDELINES FOR THE AUXILIARY EGOS

The many techniques whereby the director can involve the auxiliaries are known as "warming-up" the auxiliary ego.

Much of what is said about warming-up in Chapter 4 applies here. These techniques also apply to the warming-up of the double (see Chapter 3).

At the outset of the enactment, the protagonist can "role-reverse" (i.e., change parts) and demonstrate the behavior that the auxiliary ego is to portray. The protagonist may state the opening lines spoken by both parties. The director can then ask the protagonist in the role of the other person to show not only the other's words, but also the other person's mood, posture, tone of voice, and nonverbal behavior.

From the moment the auxiliary is selected, he should be encouraged to move right into the role, acting in the here-and-now. For example, if a group member is picked to be the protagonist's mother, she may begin talking even as she moves onto the stage: "Look at you! You're so thin! Doesn't your wife feed you?"

The auxiliary should play his hunches, take risks, and follow the cues of the director and the protagonist. If the protagonist corrects him, the auxiliary should change set quickly, for example:

PROTAGONIST: No, my mother is different, she only talks about herself.
AUXILIARY EGO: (changing set) Oh, Bill, why haven't you written me?! You know how lonely I am. . . .
PROTAGONIST: (nods his head, and answers) But Mom . . .

As the scene changes or parts are reversed, the auxiliary ego is instructed to repeat the last spoken line in his role, for example:

PROTAGONIST: (as mother) Why haven't you written?
AUXILIARY EGO: (as protagonist) Well . . .
DIRECTOR: (interrupting, to let protagonist answer for himself) Change parts. (They change places on the stage.)
AUXILIARY EGO: (as mother, repeats last line) Why haven't you written?
PROTAGONIST: Mom, I wrote you last month!
AUXILIARY EGO: (carrying on) Last month is too long, etc.

The director should consider briefing the auxiliary ego as to his role, or have the protagonist brief the auxiliary to the side while the director keeps the attention of the group.

Smoking should be prohibited on stage in order to free the participants' hands for dramatic gesture or action.

The auxiliary can be asked to bring up his own chair or prop, thus mobilizing his activity.

The auxiliary can be helped by yet another auxiliary who doubles for him; this technique thus warms up the auxiliary ego.

The auxiliary ego should be told to follow the director's directions, which may be spoken out loud or whispered to him.

If the protagonist tends to drop out-of-role, the auxiliary should address him as if he were still "in-role:" "How dare you turn your back on your mother!" The auxiliary may even grab the protagonist's arm.

The protagonist should be checked with occasionally to see if the auxiliary ego is playing the scene with reasonable accuracy. If the auxiliary cannot satisfy the protagonist's sense of how the role is to be played, the director should feel free to dismiss the auxiliary and use someone else.

A scene can be staged that precedes the main scene in time or logical sequence, for example, the "employer" plays a brief scene in which he receives information from another auxiliary, the "foreman," about the "employee" regarding the protagonist's difficulties in work; following this, the confrontation between protagonist and employer can be staged.

SUMMARY

The auxiliary ego's function is to play a variety of roles in the protagonist's enactment. The auxiliary's behavior and confrontation provoke the protagonist into a deeper involvement in the here-and-now of the drama. The effective use of the auxiliary ego can heighten the power of any action approach.

REFERENCES

Corsini, R. J. (1954). Behind your back technique. *Group Psychotherapy, 6,* 102–109.

Loeffler, F. J., & Weinstein, H. M. (1954). The co-therapist method: Problems and advantages. *Group Psychotherapy, 6,* 189.

Moreno, Z. T. (1958). Reluctant audience technique. *Group Psychotherapy, 11*(1), 278–282.

Moreno, Z. T. (1978). The function of the auxiliary ego in psychodrama with special reference to psychotic patients. *Group Psychotherapy, Psychodrama & Sociometry, 31,* 163–166.

Perls, F. S. (1969). *Gestalt therapy verbatim.* Lafayette, Calif.: Real People Press.

Toeman, Z. (1946). The auxiliary ego, double, and mirror techniques. *Sociometry, 9,* 178.

Zinger, N. (1975). A working paper for group auxiliary egos. *Group Psychotherapy & Psychodrama, 28,* 152–156.

3

The Double

The double technique consists of the use of an auxiliary ego in the specialized role of playing the part of the inner self of the protagonist. The double is occasionally called the *alter ego* by some directors. Because the expression of the protagonist's deepest emotions can be one of the major purposes of the use of psychodramatic methods, and because the use of the double is the most effective technique in bringing out emotions, role reversal is "the heart of psychodrama."

FUNCTIONS

In general, the purpose of the double is to stimulate interaction by facilitating the portrayal of the protagonist's psychological experience to its fullest range. This function may be fulfilled in many ways, which will be described later.

A second major function is to provide support for the protagonist, which helps him to take more risks and enter the interaction more completely.

A third function of the double technique is to be a vehicle for giving more effective suggestions and interpretations to the protagonist. If the auxiliary playing the double role has built a bridge of rapport through his behavior, the protagonist is relatively open to accepting and considering statements made by the double as if part of his own self were speaking. Of course, it is imperative that the director establish the norm in which the protagonist is free to disagree with, modify, or expand on the double's statement.

This empathy function of doubling can be used in many settings. For example, in individual or family therapy, I may present an interpretation-of-sorts in the following format:

"I may not be right, but I have a hunch of what you may be experiencing in that situation . . . now I'm going to be you, (John, the protagonist) and speak what you may be feeling—but you must correct me as to how it can be closer to what you're feeling . . ." (then I go into the content): "Here I am reading my paper and Sandy barges in—that really irritates me!" and so on.

This is equivalent to my role-reversing with the protagonist, without expecting him to take my role. I call it "active empathy"—it is very like Rogerian feedback, only somewhat dramatized. Instead of saying, "I'm hearing that you're feeling . . .," the therapist becomes the protagonist and then invites the protagonist to correct the "performance." This approach can be readily adapted to family therapy.

THE TECHNIQUE OF THE DOUBLE

The double is selected in the same way as the other auxiliary egos (see Chapter 2). The director introduces the double to the protagonist as follows:

"Consider this person your double, your invisible self, your alter ego with whom you may talk at times, but who exists only within yourself. He may say things that you may be feeling—things you would be hesitant to express. If his statements represent your true feelings, repeat that statement in your interaction. (See example, Chapter 5, p. 63.)

"If what the double says is not an expression of your

feelings, you are free to correct him, to say 'no.' This will negate what he says. He is then to try to better approximate your emotional state and will try to help you express your feelings and thoughts more openly. If you, the protagonist, feel the double is unable to empathize with you, you may indicate this, and we will replace him."

The director may use either of two minor variations of the technique: (1) only the protagonist may respond to what the double says, and if the double's statement is to be answered by the other people in the drama, the protagonist must repeat it; or (2) what the double says is spoken so that all may hear and it may be considered an open expression of the protagonist's feelings, unless specifically contradicted by the protagonist.

The former variant, in which the protagonist must repeat the double's statements, reinforces the necessity for the protagonist to take responsibility for what transpires and is indicated for use with more passive protagonists. The latter variant, in which what the double says may be answered directly by the others, has the advantage of speeding up the interaction.

As with the role of the auxiliary ego, there is no requirement that the person chosen to play the double resemble the actual person he portrays. "There is no age, sex, status, or race in psychodrama," says Moreno. (It is true that protagonists often pick people who resemble the real person for auxiliary ego parts, but this is not necessary.) Under any circumstances, if the auxiliary behaves even somewhat true to role, the protagonist fully accepts him in-role—even as mother, wife, or double.

If there is role reversal in the enactment, the double should take on whatever role the protagonist is involved in. Throughout the enactment the double should continue to speak in the first person: "I think," "I feel . . ." and never (to the protagonist) "you think . . .".

KINDS OF DOUBLING

In helping to express emotions, the double can emphasize or amplify statements made by the protagonist. If the double stresses that the protagonist is feeling something strongly but is not expressing those affects, the double may speak out and ventilate the anger, love, or whatever is experienced (Leveton, 1977).

A good example of this occurred during a multiple-family therapy group at a community mental health center where a daughter lashed out at her father, accusing him of being unfair and stating that she hated him. He trembled, but with his characteristic efforts at self-control, responded "Why do you hate me?" The double stood behind him and shouted, "You damn bitch! You're humiliating me! I'm trying to be controlled, but, oh, that hurt! I want you to love me!" At this, the father wept and agreed with the double, and the interaction proceeded at a more intense pace. Other ways of doubling are as follows:

Dramatizing the feelings. An extension of the first approach of doubling is the principle of maximizing the emotional content of an attitude. Thus if the protagonist says, "I like you," the double can say, "I need you"; "I'm irritated" becomes, "I hate you." Obviously, this approach should be used only when it seems that the maximizing expression is either accurate or would be productive in clarifying the protagonist's feelings.

Verbalizing nonverbal communications. Here the double begins to add more "content" to the self-system of the protagonist. If the protagonist smiles ingratiatingly, the double responds, "Why must I smile when I speak to him?" A tense jaw or clenched fist may be verbalized as, "This is getting me angry" (Taylor, 1983).

Physicalizing words and gestures. The double extends himself to hug, cling, shove, or push the other auxiliary egos in the interaction. He may strike a pillow, cringe in a crouching position, or stand on a chair to speak. This is dramatization in the nonverbal sphere.

Support. The double reinforces the protagonist's right to his feelings: "Dammit! Why should I live up to your expectations?" or, "I don't buy that load of crap!"; "It's okay if I *feel* like this!"

Questioning the self. The double questions the protagonist's attitude; again, this must be used with discretion: "Maybe I'm kidding myself . . ." or, "Is that how I really feel?"

Contradicting the feelings. The double contradicts the protagonist, but only if he wants to evoke a reinforced statement or if he believes the protagonist's self-system includes a stance opposite to his statement: "Y'know, I don't really feel this way at all!"; "I don't hate you . . . I need you!"; or, "I hate you *and* I love you!"

Defending against the feelings. The double actively verbalizes the paradigms of the protagonist's habitual defense mechanisms: Denial: "This can't be happening!" Isolation: "I don't feel a thing." Projection: "I would never feel toward you the way you feel toward me." Displacement: "Dammit! Someone's got to take the blame!!" and so forth.

Self-observation. The double notes the protagonist's general situation by introducing some comment on the protagonist's behavior: "I seem to be getting more tense"; "Oh-oh, I'm explaining again."

Related to this is the noting of emotions in the here-and-now: "I'm talking about the past, but I'm feeling embarrassed now." The double can also act as a counselor: "Say . . . I'm reacting as if he's judging me!"

Interpretation. The double must be very sensitive in his introduction of materials that are outside the protagonist's awareness. Commenting on what is *not* being said is one form: "I'm not saying anything about Dad . . . just talking to

Mom!" Referring to past incidents or other issues is another form of interpretation: "I used to feel this way as a kid!"

Interpretation of carry-over to other relationships. An important variable to be remembered is that at times the protagonist is responding to those in his enactment on two levels: not only in terms of who the other person as auxiliary is portraying (father, employer, etc.), but also in terms of who the auxiliary is in real life. For example, if the auxiliary role of father is being played by the person who is also the protagonist's therapist in other settings, the statements of the protagonist may reflect not only feelings toward the father, but also feelings toward the therapist. (This is a kind of reverse transference.) For example, in one session, the protagonist was expressing a series of demands to his "father." The double then added: "—and I'm not only saying this to you as my father, but also as my *therapist!*" This led to the protagonist's agreement and a further shift of scene toward a reevaluation of the therapist–patient relationship.

This kind of doubling can be applied to the generalization of other feelings, irrespective of who plays the other auxiliary roles: for example, "I'm frightened of you . . . I'm frightened of everybody!" or "I've felt this way with all women!"

Satire. The use of humor in psychotherapy and in doubling may be one of the most delicate arts, but at times can be very effective: "Yeah, I *want* it! I want love *and* guarantees *and* obedience!" or, "Of course I don't resent it! I like being put down!"

The use of satire, opposition, and provocation in doubling can add power to an enactment if used with sensitivity and the proper timing. Without the "art," the use of shock only leads to dissonance. The stubborn double who believes that he is making "an interpretation" when he repeatedly reinforces his statement to the repeated denials by the protagonist is only making a fool of himself or hurting the protagonist.

Divided double. Here the double is assigned to play a specific role or part of the protagonist's psyche, usually made explicit by the director. The double may be the "obedient" or the "defiant" part; the "self-blaming" or the "externalizing, self-justifying" part. This frees the protagonist to clarify his feelings about the other complementary attitudes. In this technique the director may have more than one double for different parts of the protagonist. Thus two or three doubles may be on stage.

Multiple doubles. The director may allow several people to express their feelings to the protagonist as doubles. Whereas the auxiliary as a *divided double* plays one "complex" or *part* of the protagonist's psyche, as a *multiple double,* each auxiliary doubles for the protagonist as a whole person. This technique is even more effective in sociodrama, or if the protagonist is enacting an issue that involves others deeply. Again, it must be emphasized that it is still the protagonist's feelings that must be clarified.

An extension of the multiple double is the *group or collective* double: This simply throws the interaction open to the audience and has them shout their double statements (always in the first person tense) from the floor.

The auxiliary's double. Not only can the protagonist have a double, but so may the others in the enactment. On the stage may be the protagonist, his double, his "wife" (played by an auxiliary), *her* double (played by a third auxiliary), and possibly other roles and *their doubles* and so on (see Figure 3). This technique helps those playing the other roles in the enactment to express their feelings more effectively.

Soliloquy. The double can be with the protagonist even when there is no specific interpersonal interaction, that is, when enacting a soliloquy. Examples would be "on the way home" scenes; "getting ready for bed," or simply walking

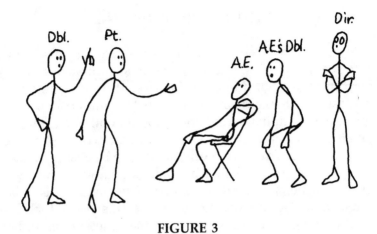

FIGURE 3

around the stage with one's double, "talking to oneself out loud."

Doubling for audience. A double may be assigned to help the audience express its feelings, positive or negative, toward the events on the stage or any of the participants in the enactment, including the director.

For example, in a drama that had become "bogged down" in overintellectualized verbosity, the audience double stood behind some group members and stated, "I'm getting bored . . . I want to help Mary reach out." This approach may catalyze a reaction, which, in turn, may further the action in the drama.

Doubling in the warm-up. From the outset, the double can be used to help the protagonist move toward readiness for action on the stage.

For example, the director is talking to a potential protagonist, and the trained auxiliary moves behind that "protagonist" and begins to double: "Say, this is embarrassing, having the director put *me* on the spot . . . I thought I would just observe . . .".

SOME SUGGESTIONS FOR DOUBLING

The tasks of helping another person to express his feelings may seem imposing, but there are some approaches that can help the potential double in his role. It is not true that an extensive historical background must be understood before one person can make inferences about another's feelings. A great deal of information is easily available from some very obvious cues. The double cannot hope to be absolutely accurate, but he will find that he is empathizing "correctly" in over half the statements he makes if he simply talks about three areas of the protagonist's life: his nonverbal communications, his use of words, and the general roles and role transitions in which the protagonist finds himself. I will describe how the double can draw inferences from these dimensions in this section, and then suggest some exercises that can be used to practice the skill of doubling.

The first group of cues for the double comes from the protagonist's *nonverbal communications*. By imitating the protagonist's posture, expression, gesture, and voice tone, the double finds himself experiencing the same kinds of body sensations as the subject. These sensations act as somasthetic cues that provide the double with a wealth of intuitive information about how the subject feels (Deutsch, 1960, 1963). For example, if a double were to imitate a protagonist who is slumped in his chair, the sensation of the distribution of weight in that posture might suggest to the double the quality of the feeling of the subject (e.g., it might help the double to discern whether the protagonist is sulking, or if he is really depressed). I would suggest that the reader try out the following: unobtrusively imitate others, and to a surprising extent you find yourselves "feeling" as they do (Krainen, 1972).

The best physical position for the double is to place himself behind, slightly to the side of, and facing the protagonist at about a 30 degree angle. From this vantage point he can observe and imitate his subject without being distractingly obvious. The proximity of this position may facilitate a sense of symbolic identification. Rapport may be occasionally heightened by the double's placing one hand on the protagonist's shoulder.

A second source of information for the double may be derived from the *way the protagonist uses words*. As long as the double is in the process of trying to understand his subject, he should try to get a feeling for the protagonist's "self-system." What kinds of words, what connotations, what levels of abstractions does the protagonist use? (Some knowledge of semantics is often very helpful in this regard.) In the early stages of doubling, the double should try to paraphrase what the protagonist is most consciously trying to express. Only later, after the rapport has been established, may he go on to amplify, express, dramatize, and in other ways extend the doubling to the many functions noted earlier in this chapter. In the beginning, however, the double wants to *understand*, and thus needs to listen almost uncritically. Any caricaturization of the protagonist by the double in the early phases will disrupt the relationship.

Also based on the protagonist's use of words the double can find clues as to how his subject is feeling from the *discrepancy between voice tone and content*. If the protagonist speaks in an emotion-filled voice about trivial issues, the double may be led toward thinking about what that emotion means. On the other hand, if the protagonist is speaking in a flat, effectless tone about rather dramatic problems, the double may attend to (and later, comment on) the defense mechanism of isolation of emotion.

The third major technique for the double's building an empathic awareness of the protagonist is *to assess the protagonist's roles and obvious characteristics*. These can be divided into several categories: (1) physical features, (2) stage in life, and (3) the challenges, advantages, and disadvantages of any present or imminent life roles. The double should assess these obvious or easily accessible conditions. It is not necessary for the double to feel he must have the "whole story" in order to make inferences about these roles, since the relationship is such that he can interact mutually and, if he errs, he can easily be corrected. Nevertheless, the double will find that a surprisingly high proportion of his inferences will be accurate. Each accurate response of the double develops his rapport with the protagonist while an inaccurate response does *not* alienate him unless it is extreme or humiliating.

For example, an auxiliary ego may make a number of statements in the double role that might be part of the situation of anyone who has a physical characteristic that is different from most of the people in his social situation: a different or minority ethnic, racial, or religious affiliation; being tall or short, overweight or thin; having any disfiguring scars or unusual features; and so on. What does a man feel when his hairline begins to recede? What special issues concern someone who is short?

The double can similarly make any comments that would be shared by most people at the following stages in life: the man about to retire; the person being told he has a serious illness; the feelings and anxieties that accompany a promotion; the mixed feelings of being a new parent; and so forth.

Related to the issue of role transition are the groups of feelings that accompany most life roles in the sexual, family, vocational, social, and financial areas. What could any double say about the following situations?: The man who reaches his fiftieth birthday and whose income and status have not met his expectations; the woman in her thirties who finds that her husband has recently been unfaithful; or the young man who feels himself falling into a vocational rut.

The double can thus utilize the inferences that any person can make about a situation or quality, if he will give himself permission to take the risk of playing his hunches out loud.

EXERCISES FOR BUILDING THE CAPACITY FOR DOUBLING

Here are some of the exercises that may be used for building empathic skills; they also are excellent warm-up techniques.

1. The group breaks into pairs. All participants are instructed to list on a piece of paper four qualities that they like about themselves and four qualities that they dislike. After the lists are made, the group members are instructed to exchange lists with their partners. All of the pairs conduct the exercise simultaneously as they sit around the room. One member of each pair starts off by reading the partner's list. After reading each item, such as, "I am overweight," the person reading the list goes on to describe how it would feel if this were a personal quality. Drawing on any actual experiences, the person speaks for about a minute, exploring the inferences that can be made regarding the item on the list— advantages, disadvantages, implications.

The partner whose list is being read is to listen but make no reply until after both have finished the exercise. When one finishes reading and commenting on the partner's list, the other does likewise. The exercise should take about 20 minutes. Only after both partners have read the other's list should they give feedback and engage in a discussion. It is unimportant whether or not the participants are correct; what is essential is the willingness to make intuitive inferences based on the qualities noted on the lists.

2. A similar exercise for a small group is "secret pooling." Each group member writes a "secret" on a piece of paper.

The secret should be about something which the person would feel quite uncomfortable revealing to the group. The papers are all folded in the same fashion and mixed thoroughly with those of the others in the group to ensure anonymity. When the papers are redistributed members check quickly to make sure they didn't pick their own secrets. Then, in turn, each person reads out the secret as if it were *a personal secret*. All participants speak in the first person and go on to explain (making inferences and taking risks of interpretation) how it feels to have that secret as part of one's own life history. Each person speaks for about a minute, talking about the feelings and attitudes that are associated with the contents of the secret.

It is often surprising and relieving to group members to find that others talk about their anonymously written secrets with empathy and kindness; the commonness of themes is also usually striking in this exercise. Through the discovery of shared feelings about emotional issues, the group moves toward greater group cohesion. This exercise thus serves many functions in developing empathic skills as well as serving as a warm-up for further group activities.

3. A more playful exercise is the "directed-fantasy double." The director speaks to the group as follows: "Think of an object, animal, or character in fairytale—and then become that thing. What is your future? Past?" The more you do this, the more you will be ready to empathically move into a variety of roles.

SUMMARY

The auxiliary ego and, in particular, the double are distinguishing characteristics of psychodramatic enactment that are contributions to the field of action approaches in psychotherapy and education. In particular, the double role provides not only a powerful stimulus to the protagonist, but, equally importantly, offers an opportunity for building the empathic skills of role reversal in the person who doubles.

REFERENCES

Deutsch, F. (1960). Entering the mind through the sensory gateways in associative anamnesis. *Psychosomatic Medicine, 22*(6), 466–480.

Deutsch, F. (Spring 1963). Analytic posturology and synesthesiology. *Psychoanalytic Review, 50,* 40–67.

Ferreira, A. (1961). Empathy and the bridge function of the ego, *Journal of American Psychoanalytic Association, 9*(1), 91–105.

Goldstein, S. (1967). Effects of doubling on involvement in group psychotherapy. *Psychotherapy: Theory, Research and Practice, 4*(2), 57–60.

Katz, R. L. (1963). *Empathy—Its nature and use.* New York: Free Press.

Krainen, J. M. (1972). Counter-playing: A group therapy technique. *American Journal of Psychiatry, 129* (5): 600–601.

Leveton, E. (1977). *Psychodrama for the timid clinician.* New York: Springer Publishing Co.

Ossorio, A., & Fine, L. (1960). Psychodrama as a catalyst for social change in a mental hospital, In J. Masserman and J. L. Moreno (Eds.) *Reviews and integrations,* Volume 5 of *Progress in psychotherapy.* New York: Grune and Stratton.

Perrott, L. A. (1975). Doubling from an existential-phenomenological viewpoint. *Group Psychotherapy & Psychodrama, 28,* 66–69.

Taylor, G. (1983). The effect of nonverbal doubling on the emotional response of the double. *Journal of Group Psychotherapy, Psychodrama, & Sociometry, 36*(2), 61–68.

Toeman, Z. (1946). The auxiliary ego, double, and mirror techniques, *Sociometry, 9,* 178.

Toeman, Z. (1948). The double situation in psychodrama. *Sociatry, 1*(4), 436–448.

Walstedt, J. (1968). Teaching empathy. *Mental Hygiene, 52*(4), 600–611.

4

The Warm-Up

The *warm-up*, in its more restricted sense, refers to the first phase of a psychodramatic enactment in which a protagonist is helped to become involved enough to move into action. In a broader sense, *warming up* is an important psychological phenomenon that is all too often neglected. To *warm up* to any activity requires the gradual increase of physical movement, the inclusion of spontaneous behaviors, and the direction of attention toward some specific idea or task. The principles of warming up apply not only to structuring the first stage of any psychodramatic involvement, but also to many areas of everyday life. This chapter will focus primarily on the practical aspects of using warming up techniques in psychodrama.

The most important issue in warming up is the establishment of a context that fosters *spontaneity*. The necessary conditions for spontaneous behavior include (1) a sense of trust and safety; (2) norms that allow for the inclusion of nonrational and intuitive dimensions; (3) some feeling of tentative distance, which is one element of playfulness; and (4) a movement toward risk taking and exploration into novelty. The theory of spontaneity has been written about at length by Moreno and others, and supplemental reading in these and related articles is recommended (Blatner, 1988).

The first phase of any group activity involves the development of some concensus as to the purposes, methods, duration, dimensions, and division of responsibilities in the group. Let's consider them. For example, the group leader is a woman who starts by identifying herself and facilitates introductions. Often the group leader, whom we will now call the director, talks with the group, the process of clarification of the task begins to unfold.

THE DIRECTOR'S WARM-UP

The director is best able to function in the use of psychodramatic methods only if she is warmed up. To achieve this she should be physically active in walking about, moving chairs, talking with the group about a variety of topics, presenting a basic introduction regarding what she will be doing, how long the group will last, and so forth. All these activities build a dynamic and imaginative warm-up in herself (see Figure 4). Few things are more counterproductive to a group's warming up than a director who talks with the group from a sitting position.

During her own warm-up, the director is developing spontaneity in herself. This is her way of disclosing some of her own style. If she can communicate a sense of authenticity and warmth, her warming up begins to allow the group to know and trust her (Sacks, 1967). Her behavior further models for the group the norms of self-disclosure, spontaneity, acceptance of humor, toleration of some distance (i.e., the acceptability of some reserve on the part of the group members and a respect for some unwillingness to engage in significant self-disclosure at first), and the acceptability of action and forceful expression. The director is meanwhile interacting with the group, and developing a level of *tele* with them. *Tele* is Moreno's term for a multileveled, multi-

FIGURE 4

directional sense of relationship: a term richer than rapport and more mutual than transference and countertransference.

Of course, during this first phase the director is also mentally warming up to the task that lies ahead. She must be able to assess the many factors that could affect the group process: a skill that only comes with extensive experience and reading (see Chapter 10).

The director must also become aware of her own resistances to the group, if any are present. A common way in which a director might experience resistance to the group lies in her own lack of preparation or in the presence of any artificial expectations she may have. Does the director feel she must "put on a show"? Does she have stereotyped attitudes toward some of the group members? Does she wish she could avoid dealing with the group's stereotypes of herself?

The director may cope with these mixed feelings and expectations of herself using several techniques, all of which facilitate her own warming-up: (1) she may discuss her plans and apprehensions in advance with a co-worker; (2) she may review her own tolerance for not needing a "dramatic happening" to occur as part of her introduction to the group, thus clarifying her own position at the outset; or (3) she may allow her own *negative tele* to be first on the agenda for the group discussion or psychodrama (Moreno, Z., 1958). Of course, if a director feels a great deal of overinvolvement, she should decline to direct, and if another potential director is available, that person should be allowed to take over the leadership role.

GROUP COHESION

In the next phase, following the basic self-introduction and her own warm-up, the director helps to develop group cohesion. The first step in building a sense of group identity and trust is to get the group members to know each other. The director may choose to employ a variety of introductory exercises. She can modify these exercises to meet the purposes of the group task:

The director asks each member to find a partner to get to know. Then, in a few minutes she asks each of the group members to introduce the partner to the group. Partners may be chosen as people one knows, strangers, someone who seems very different from oneself, someone with whom one has felt some conflict, or one's spouse. A series of these *dyads* may be structured in order to have each group member not only meet but experience something different with each partner, thus consolidating the partner's name in memory. Some nonverbal exercises can be included in these dyads: "talking" with hands or backs, trust walks, and so forth. (In the *trust walk* or *blind walk*, one partner takes the blindfolded other on a little tour, emphasizing the awareness of trust issues.)

By the use of *self-presentation,* group members are asked to introduce themselves and to say something about their backgrounds, expectations, and the like.

The use of action exercises early in the group's development may blend into the use of other structured experiences that are designed not only as introductions, but also as steps in building trust, self-disclosure, and playfulness. They are also useful as an introduction to a variety of modalities, such as guided imagination and nonverbal communication.

GROUP TASK AND WARM-UP TECHNIQUES

The usè of action exercises or structured experiences not only works toward the task of building group cohesion, but also serves to sensitize group members to those dimensions of their personalities with which they have the greatest conflict—their "blind spots." I find that about one-fifth of any group is unaffected by any given exercise; another fifth is quite affected—the technique really arouses an awareness of some conflict area; and the rest of the group is mildly affected. After several exercises, most of the group members become more aware of their own problems.

At this point, the director moves into developing a theme or finding a protagonist. If the group is warming up slowly, or the director would like to start at some distance, the discussion of some topic of general interest may come next. Some further techniques include:

1. In groups that already know each other, the director may simply wait in the background while the group warms itself up, discussing and joking about a variety of topics. Often a common theme emerges after several minutes, which the director may capitalize on by turning it into an enactment. This approach is called the *undirected warm-up*.

2. If the group knows its own task, the director simply starts with a discussion, or uses a concrete example with which to explore sociodramatically some of the issues. This would be called a *directed warm-up* (Yablonsky & Enneis, 1956).

After the group has developed some group cohesion, the

director discusses the group theme at a distance, using situations which are somewhat removed from real life. Some of these warm-ups include:

3. *The melodrama.* A group member could possibily be the director. The members could then have "auditions" for the various parts: heroine, hero, villain, heroine's mother, father, or others; the basic plot is that the mortgage is to be foreclosed unless the heroine gives herself to the villain; the sawmill or railroad tracks scenes follow; then the rescue. Improvisations and "hamming it up" are encouraged. Fairy tales and myths can also be enacted.

4. *Situation tests.* For individuals or groups. Examples include: the "lifeboat"—who will be chosen to die?; "left on a desert island"—how will the group organize itself?; "the stranger in the town restaurant"; "the employment interview"; and so on. A range of dramatic, fantasied, humorous, tragic, or frustrating situations, from slight to extreme, can be used.

5. *The magic shop.* This is an especially useful technique. The director has the group imagine a small shop on the stage. The shopkeeper may be played by a trained auxiliary, a member of the group, or even by the director. The group is told that on the shelves of this magic shop all types of wonderful qualities can be found. Anyone who wishes to buy may come into the shop. Eventually someone volunteers to become the customer–protagonist.

The customer's first requests are often quite vague: I want "love," "wisdom," "immortality," "success," etc. As the first task, the shopkeeper engages the customer in a discussion in order to clarify more specifically what's wanted, for example, from whom does the customer want love? What conditions will be accepted? This conversation should remain within the metaphor of a shopkeeper simply trying to understand what is desired. The more general the desire, the more expensive or inexpensive it may be: "You want love from *everybody?* Well, that will cost quite a bit more," says the shopkeeper.

The negotiation of the price comprises the second task within the technique of the magic shop. Money cannot be offered. The shopkeeper explains that the only barter can be some quality or facet of the customer's life or personality that will be surrendered—something that someone *else* might wish to buy some day from the magic shop. The price offered often leads to some thought-provoking challenges:

CUSTOMER: I'll give up my selfishness for love!
SHOPKEEPER: Are you willing to give up *all* of your selfishness?
CUSTOMER: Well now . . .

The director may allow either the protagonist or the auxiliary–shopkeeper to consult with the audience for their advice. What would be a fair price for immortality?

Often a customer will claim an inability to think of something to offer as payment. (The statement, "I don't know," betrays a passive-dependent stance and should be redefined as, "I'm having difficulty thinking of something.") This situation not only demonstrates the protagonist's passive style, but also can be a starting point from which to explore the protagonist's lack of awareness of inner resources.

Once the tentative bargain has been struck, the protagonist is encouraged to try out the newly purchased qualities, or to show how it feels to get along without the quality that was just given up. In these follow-up symbolic enactments, the protagonist may find that there is a greater need than previously realized for what was given up; or, on the other hand, that what was purchased is not what was expected. For example, the man who wanted an agreeable wife found that he was bored by the enactment of his "ideal" mate. The girl who would give up "being controlling" felt too vulnerable when she had to enact a situation blindfolded.

In summary, the magic shop is an excellent technique not only for warming-up a group, but also for the purposes of clarifying goals and examining the consequences of one's choices.

6. *Guided fantasy* refers to a wide variety of exercises in which the director has the group members imagine a variety of general themes, the details of which are filled in by each individual's unique imagery. Picturing trips through one's own body, journeys through forests, mountains, houses, or into the sea—are all common themes. This technique has also been called the *directed daydream* method, and has become a major approach within the general school of psychosynthesis. The group can utilize these methods individually, while working in dyads, or they can share a fantasy together as a group. The works of Leuner, Assagioli, Desoille, and Gerard have all received increasing recognition in this area (Leuner, 1969).

Another major group of warm-ups are those derived from the related fields of the creative arts therapies.

7. *Theater games* and exercises from the mime can be adapted as warm-ups for psychodramatic enactments. Activities derived from creative dramatics are widely utilized in school settings and can easily lead to explorations of more meaningful issues (Spolin, 1963).

8. *Dance* and all the exercises that lead to spontaneity and involvement in expressiveness can easily be part of any warm-up. Related to the field of dance are the activities derived from body movement, sensory awakening, bioenergetics, and rhythmical group rituals. Simple voiced intonations—chants, grunts, repetitive noises—can all be added to emphasize breathing and expressive action. These warm-ups not only generate a great deal of readiness for action, but also establish a norm of physical involvement within the group.

9. *Music* can be used in a variety of ways. The group members can create and/or play simple instruments in an improvisatory style. The interplay can be heightened by a mixture of making music, voice sounds, and body movement. The introduction of simple musical instruments, elementary circle dance, and stretching activities is especially valuable in working with patients who have been passive or institutionalized for long periods (Chace, 1945).

Background music may also be an effective catalyst to group interaction. The lyrics of many contemporary songs can suggest common emotional themes for group discussion. A trained music therapist can provide different moods in music which will accompany and heighten the flow of action in many enactments (J. J. Moreno, 1980).

10. *Artistic materials* can be adapted to a group setting. Paints, clay, papier-mâché, pastels, crayons, finger paints, colored sand, and a wide variety of collage materials are all useful in this regard. Starting with ideas derived from art therapy, the group can move from the creative media to enactments and then back to further involvement in artistic creation.

One example of the use of artistic materials is *shared drawings:* in a couples group, each pair is asked to create a picture together, without using any words; the drawing is to represent their relationship. About 15 minutes are allotted for this, and then the director has each couple in turn display and discuss its picture.

All of the above-mentioned approaches can become warm-up techniques that emphasize spontaneity and a validation of the creative dimensions within the self.

Finally, each director will undoubtedly improvise a variety of modifications of any of the above-mentioned techniques. James Sacks, for example, combines elements of many different approaches in one of his warm-ups: The group members form a fairly tight circle, sitting on cushions or low seats. The director asks them to lean forward; in turn members state their names (or nicknames) and mention what they hope to achieve in the group session. *All* of these statements are to be no greater than one sentence in length. Other directions follow: "Share with the group something they don't know about you; tell an old, old memory; name someone with whom you have unfinished business." At this point, the one-sentence rule may be lifted. The group members are then asked to dictate a letter to the person with whom they have unfinished business. This technique is likely to be useful in building group cohesion, encouraging self-disclosure, and developing themes and protagonists for future enactments.

THE SELECTION OF A PROTAGONIST

There are many ways in which a protagonist may emerge out of the group process:

1. The protagonist may volunteer in that or an earlier session. The director may want to have the group vote on whom is to be dealt with if there are several volunteers, or she may arbitrarily choose in what order they will be protagonists.
2. The director may simply wait quietly until someone does volunteer, but the director has to know where to use this approach or it may backfire. Some groups will simply not respond.
3. The protagonist may be preselected by the therapists.
4. The director may walk around and converse with different people in the group until she finds someone who is ready to be the protagonist; or she may try a common warm-up,

FIGURE 5

such as the "auxiliary chair," and see who emerges as the most likely candidate.

5. The protagonist may emerge out of the natural ongoing group process. This occurs when the group arrives and is catalyzed into some natural joking or discussion of a topic. This spontaneity should not be suppressed by an unspoken or explicit "let's get down to business," which has the effect of a wet blanket on a fire. People do not like to talk about their problems: it is humiliating, and such a suggestion invariably quenches spontaneity in a group. Instead, the director should wait. She may even go along with the joking, trusting that she can gently turn it into a meaningful issue. Eventually both a theme and a protagonist emerge (Kumar & Treadwell, 1986).

6. The director, especially in work or school situations, may start with a short talk on some general theme. If it is controversial, so much the better. The group may find itself agreeing or disagreeing, and this can then be made explicit by setting up a spectrogram (see p. 113).

7. Using spectrograms, sociodramas, or other group-centered methods, a protagonist may emerge as one who is

especially concerned about something triggered in the discussion. In addition, in order to stimulate a protagonist, or to help him become more involved in his life situation, the director can use more individual-centered warm-ups:

8. *The auxiliary chair.* This is a major warm-up method and can also be used at times during the action session (Lippitt, 1958). The director puts forward an empty chair and says, "There is someone sitting in this chair—someone important to you. Visualize him or her, what s/he is doing, wearing, what s/he might be thinking about, etc . . . When it's clear to you, raise your hand." Then when most have indicated they have seen someone, the director may proceed to ask whom they see in the chair. The director may ask no one in particular and wait for volunteers, or address her question to a specific person. When someone responds, he is either asked to be that person (and sit in the chair) or is asked what he has to say to whomever he sees in the chair. This can lead to a brief interchange, which may lead to a further enactment.

During an enactment, the auxiliary chair can also be used when the protagonist has difficulty relating to a real person. The chair in this sense becomes the major instrument in monodrama. (See Figure 2, p. 24.)

9. *The action sociogram.* In this method, originated by J. L. Moreno, the protagonist presents his "social atom"—the key people most relevant to his experience (often his family) as if they were a group of sculptures in a diorama, or a three-dimensional painting (see Figure 6). Members of the group become auxiliary egos and portray these significant figures. With the help of the director, the protagonist positions them in characteristic poses that symbolically portray their essential relationship to the protagonist (who is also portrayed within the scene by an auxiliary). The use of the posture, the direction in which each figure faces, and the proximity or distance from the protagonist in the scene may all sym-

FIGURE 6

bolically represent the quality of the relationship. Finally, the protagonist gives each figure in the scene a characteristic sentence or phrase to speak, which symbolically brings them "to life." He then steps back and observes, or enters the scene and begins to relate to his family or central group (Seabourne, 1963).

Another variant of the action sociogram is for the director to use physical objects to represent the social atom: a group of coins of various denominations; a chess set; or a set of hand puppets (preferably of animals). The protagonist is instructed to identify the chessman or hand puppet of his choice with one of the people in his social atom. It is often interesting for example, to watch a protagonist pick the mouse hand puppet or the pawn for the father; the bear puppet or bishop for the brother, and so forth. Which figure, where it is placed, and what it does can then lead to an extrapolation from the symbolic situation to the dynamics of the protagonist's social atom (Schwab, 1978; Taylor, 1984).

FIGURE 7

MOVING INTO ACTION

After the protagonist has emerged from the group, the last phase of the warm-up remains. The basic issue is discussed with the protagonist. "Yes, that issue troubles me," is the essence of the contract. "Let's work on it," says the director, and the protagonist is led gently by the hand to the staging area.

Depending on his readiness, the protagonist may sit at the second level-edge of the stage, and the director sits with him (Figure 7). Often the director and protagonist stand or walk around in the staging area as they discuss the issue in order to arrive at a specific example: a place or a person. At this point the enactment moves to the third level of the stage, if one is being used.

The director takes an appropriate cue that points to an enactment and suggests it. If a name of someone who seems important to the protagonist is mentioned, possibly an interaction with that person is to be the "first scene." If a time of life is mentioned, the director moves toward a specific memory or image.

During the warm-up, the protagonist is helped to engage in increasing activity. When a protagonist is warmed up to an unusually high pitch he will almost direct the drama by himself.

If, during the warm-up, the protagonist shows increasing anxiety that is manifested by resistance, the director must shift the enactment into a less emotionally loaded sphere of exploration while still continuing the action. This is similar to the process of desensitization by imagery and relaxation in the treatment of phobic patients: If the client indicates that he is picturing a scene that makes him too tense, the therapist allows him to return to a less frightening image with which he can relax, but the therapy continues. Similarly, if the protagonist "freezes," the director may ask him to soliloquize, or to use one of the following warm-ups.

Hand puppets. A puppet show can often be an effective warm-up, while giving the protagonist some distance (Kors, 1964). The use of masks may have a similar function (Bringham, 1970).

Blackout. The entire theater is blacked out although all actions continue as if there would be full daylight. This is done so that the protagonist may go through a painful experience unobserved, and so the protagonist can retain the experience of solitude.

Turn your back. A protagonist is occasionally embarrassed to present a particular episode while facing the group. He is then permitted to turn his back to the group and to act as if he were alone, in his own home, or wherever the episode takes place. Once the protagonist has reached a sufficient degree of involvement, he is then ready to carry on facing the audience.

Portrayal of a dream. This offers an excellent first enactment for a protagonist's exploration of his problem. It is often used in Gestalt therapy (Fielding, 1967).

Hypnodrama. The protagonist is hypnotized and then helped to enact his situation in a hypnotic state (Enneis, 1950; Moreno J. L., 1950).

After a sufficient warm-up, the protagonist is usually ready to enter the second phase of the psychodrama—*the action*, which will be discussed in the next chapter.

SUMMARY

The warming-up process is the first and essential part of any enactment and is based on the fundamental need for any person to *gradually* develop increasing involvement and spontaneity through goal-directed physical action. In reference to group process, the warm-up phase applies to the components of (1) the director's warm-up, (2) building group cohesion, (3) developing a group theme, (4) finding a protagonist, and (5) moving the protagonist onto the stage.

REFERENCES

Blatner, A. (1988). *Foundations of psychodrama* (Chapter 7 on spontaneity.) New York: Springer.

Bringham, F. M. (February, 1970). Masks as a psychotherapeutic modality. *Journal of American Osteopathic Association, 69,* 549–555.

Chace M., (1945). Rhythm and movement as used in St. Elizabeth's Hospital. *Sociometry, 8,* 481–483.

Corynetz, P. (1945). The warming-up process of an audience. *Sociometry, 8*(3–4), 218–225.

Enneis, J. M. (1951). The dynamics of group and action processes in therapy. *Group Psychotherapy, 4*(1), 17–21.

Enneis, J. M. (1950). The hypnodramatic technique. *Group Psychotherapy, 3*(1), 11–40.

Fielding, B. (1967). Enactment of dreams in group psychotherapy. *Psychotherapy: Theory, Research and Practice, 4*(2), 74.

Fine, L. J. (1959). Nonverbal aspects of psychodrama, In J. Masserman and J. L. Moreno (Eds.) *Social psychotherapy,* Volume 4 of *Progress in psychotherapy.* New York: Grune and Stratton,

Galper, J. (1970). Nonverbal communication exercises in groups. *Social Work, 15*(2), 68–71.

Hammer, M. (1967). The directed daydream technique. *Psychotherapy: Theory, Research and Practice, 4*(4), 173.

Kipper, D. A. (1967). On spontaneity. *Group Psychotherapy, 20*(1).

Kole, D. (1967). The spectrogram in psychodrama. *Group Psychotherapy, 20*(1–2), 53–61.

Kors, P. C. (1964). Unstructured puppet shows as group procedures in therapy with children. *Psychiatric Quarterly Supplement, 38*(1), 56–75.

Kumar, V. K. & Treadwell, T. W. (1986). Identifying a protagonist: Techniques and factors. *Journal of Group Psychotherapy, Psychodrama & Sociometry, 38*(4), 155–164.

Leuner, H. C. (1969). Guided affective imagery. *American Journal of Psychotherapy, 23*(1), 4–22.

Lippitt, R. (1958). Auxiliary chair technique. *Group Psychotherapy, 11*(1–2), 8–23.

Malamud, D. I., & Machover, S. (1965). *Toward self-understanding: Group techniques for self-confrontation.* Springfield, Ill.: Charles C Thomas.

Middleman, R. R. (1968). *The nonverbal method in working with groups.* New York: Associated Press.

Mintz, E. (1971). Therapy techniques and encounter techniques. *American Journal of Psychotherapy, 25*(1), 107.

Moreno, J. J. (1980). Musical psychodramas. A new direction in music therapy. *Journal of Music Therapy, 17*(1), 34–42.

Moreno, J. L. (1950). Hypnodrama and psychodrama. *Group Psychotherapy, 1950, 3*(1), 1–10.

Moreno, Z. T. (1958). The "reluctant therapist" and the "reluctant audience" technique in psychodrama. *Group Psychotherapy, 11,* 278–282.

Moreno, Z. T. (1959). A survey of psychodramatic techniques. *ACTA Psychotherapeutica, 7,* 197–206.

Otto, H. A. (1970). *Group methods to actualize human potential: A handbook.* Beverly Hills: Holistic Press.

Pankratz, L., & Buchan, G. (1965). Exploring psychodrama techniques with defective delinquents. *Group Psychotherapy 18*(3), 136–141.

Pfeiffer, J. W., & Jones, J. E. (1969). *Structured experience for human relations training.* Iowa City: University Associates Press, 3 vols.

Sacks, J. M. (1967). Psychodrama, the warm-up. *Group Psychotherapy, 20*(4), 118–121.

Schwab, R. (1978). Use of a chess set: An application of psychodramatic and sociometric techniques. *Group Psychotherapy, Psychodrama & Sociometry, 31,* 41–45.

Seabourne, B. (1963). The action sociogram. *Group Psychotherapy, 16*(3), 145–155.

Spolin, V. (1963). *Improvisations for the theater.* Evanston, Ill.: Northwestern University Press.

Stevens, J. A. (1971). *Awareness: Exploring, experimenting, experiencing.* Lafayette, Cal.: Real People Press.

Streitfeld, H. S., and Lewis, H. R. (1971). *Growth Games.* New York: Harcourt, Brace, Jovanovich.

Taylor, J. A. (1984). The diagnostic use of the social atom. *Journal of Group Psychotherapy, Psychodrama & Sociometry, 37*(2), 67–84.

Warner, G. D. (1970). The didactic auxiliary chair. *Group Psychotherapy, 23*(1–2), 31–34.

Weiner, H. A., & Sacks, J. M. (1969). Warm-up and sum-up. *Group Psychotherapy, 22*(1–2), 85–102.

Yablonsky, L., & Enneis, J. M. (1956). Psychodrama, theory and practice, In F. Fromm-Reichman & J. L. Moreno (Eds.) *Progress in Psychotherapy,* Vol. 1. New York: Grune and Stratton.

Zweben, J., & Hamman, K. (1970). Prescribed games: A theoretical perspective on the use of group techniques. *Psychotherapy: Theory, Research and Practice, 7*(1), 22–27.

5

The Action

This chapter will discuss the process of the second phase of the psychodrama, the *action* portion. Following the warm-up of the group and the selection of the protagonist, the director is then faced with the challenge of staging the enactment in order to most fully help the protagonist portray the psychological dimensions of his problem.

It should be noted that every psychodramatic enactment is unique—there is no fixed sequence of events. In general, however, there is a movement toward the core conflict and greater emotional expression as the drama unfolds. The different phases in the enactment vary in each case, but usually follow the order of presentation in this chapter.

PRESENTATION OF THE PROBLEM

When the protagonist is selected, he is brought toward the stage and is encouraged to describe his situation. As the director discusses the protagonist's problem, a specific example is sought. Then if the protagonist begins to narrate the situation, the director encourages him to *portray* the scene, rather than talk about what happened (Figure 8, p. 61).

FIGURE 8

PROTAGONIST: ("Joe") Well, I had this fight with my boss . . .

DIRECTOR: Show us, don't tell us. (The director gets up and invites Joe into the stage area.) Where does the scene happen? (Figure 8)

JOE: It was in the office.

DIRECTOR: It *is* in the office—it's happening *now!* Let's see the office . . . where is the boss's chair? . . . desk? . . . Are you sitting or standing? (Figure 9)

The director continues to speak in the present tense, reinforcing the protagonist's immersion in the here-and-now.

The protagonist is helped to move around the stage, visualizing the scene. The invitation to act in the here-and-now has an almost hypnotic effect: It is surprising how easily and naturally most protagonists become involved in the scene.

As the protagonist describes the scene, the director asks him to point out the furniture and comment on the textures of the materials, the colors, the weather—all concrete sensations that immerse him even more deeply in the enactment. The setting of the stage is for the protagonist's benefit, not

FIGURE 9

the audience's. It may be as brief or prolonged as the director feels is necessary in order to maximize the protagonist's continuing warm-up. He is instructed to move around the stage, positioning the chairs himself. Encouragement of the protagonist's physical action in walking and moving further increases his warm-up. It is important to maximize physical activity throughout the psychodramatic enactment in order to avoid becoming bogged down in a wordy interaction (one of the most common pitfalls of directing). Later in the psychodrama, the director continues to use a variety of scene changes, role reversals, standing on chairs, pushing, climbing over furniture, and many other techniques in order to keep up the pace of action.

BRINGING IN THE AUXILIARY

As the scene is set, the auxiliary egos are chosen and encouraged to move immediately into their roles.

FIGURE 10

DIRECTOR: Okay, let's have someone to play your boss (Figure 10).

Joe is asked to pick someone in the group (call him Bill) to be the auxiliary. Bill comes on stage and the director immediately warms him up to his role:

DIRECTOR: Mr. Jones, you asked Joe to come in today . . . he can't hear you right now . . . if you were just thinking out loud to yourself, giving a "soliloquy," let's hear what you have to say regarding why you want to see him.

AUXILIARY EGO: (Bill, as Mr. Jones) Well, Joe hasn't been performing very well at his job (Figure 11).

DIRECTOR: (glancing at Joe) Is that right?

JOE: No, that's not it . . . my work is fine.

DIRECTOR: Change parts (role-reverse) . . . Joe, be Mr. Jones and begin the encounter.

JOE: (as Mr. Jones) Look, Joe, this is the third time this week you've come in late.

DIRECTOR: Change parts and start again . . . Mr. Jones (Aside murmuring): Repeat the last line.

FIGURE 11

A.E.: (Mr. Jones) Look Joe, this is, etc . . .

JOE: But, Sir, when I took this job, we agreed that because of my having to take care of my kids my work time would be adjusted! (Figure 12).

A.E.: Well, the other employees are noticing and complaining . . .

The issues are unfolding. If the auxiliary ego does not play his part as the protagonist visualizes its essential quality, further role reversals are used to guide the auxiliary ego toward a more accurate role portrayal.

If the protagonist tends to narrate to the audience, the auxiliary should address him "in-role";

A.E.: You're talking as if I'm not even here! What's the big idea of being so late this morning!

If the protagonist becomes lost in intellectualization or confused as to his feelings, there are some other techniques that may be used:

FIGURE 12

Non-verbal. The protagonist can enact the scene without using words, using sounds without words ("blah-blah" or gibberish) or no sounds at all, simply gestures. The former induces the protagonist to increase the pace, tone, rhythm, and inflections of his voice, which exaggerates the expression of feeling without content. The latter, using no sound at all, channels him toward dramatizing his gestures and expressions, which also throws the emotional components of the interaction into sharp contrast.

Soliloquy. The protagonist is instructed to walk up and down and talk to himself out loud, in order to clarify his feelings. He can then reenter the interaction with the auxiliary ego (Mr. Jones).

Double. If the protagonist has difficulty expressing his emotions clearly, a *double* may be brought in, an auxiliary who will be Joe's inner feelings (see Figure 13 and also Chapter 3):

DIRECTOR: Mark, will you come in here. (Gives instructions for doubling, then carries on with the scene.)

JOE: (continuing) Well, Sir, I think that isn't what we agreed on . . .

FIGURE 13

MR. JONES:	Look, Joe, we have to run a business here . . .
DOUBLE:	Look, you bastard, here's how I really feel . . . (Figure 14)
JOE:	(nodding) Yeah! You can't push me around like this!
MR JONES:	Now hold on there . . .
DOUBLE:	It's about time someone was frank with you! When you make an agreement . . .
JOE:	—Yeah, you have to stand by what you say!

From this point, the interaction can be continued, replayed, or the scene shifted and a related interaction portrayed. If Joe has problems with authority, many other encounters with authority figures can be explored, always moving to more central emotional issues.

MOVING FROM PERIPHERAL TO CENTRAL

Often the protagonist is warmed up enough to begin an enactment, but the "core" conflict is still buried under explanations and descriptions of circumstances. This "resistance"

FIGURE 14

is not only to be allowed, but actually *used* in the building a preliminary scene. The director should respect the protagonist's need to start at the periphery of a problem.

For example, if the protagonist has difficulty in dealing with an emotionally loaded conflict with his mother, he may be helped to enact a similar situation with a saleslady. Another technique is to have the protagonist play the role of his own brother or sister, and to enact with his mother from that position. Marguerite Parrish (1953) wrote about the following two useful techniques:

The substitute role technique is frequently used and is helpful when working with protagonists who tend to be suspicious and resist portraying themselves on the stage. This technique was successfully used with a middle-aged woman diagnosed as having involutional melancholia with some paranoid traits. She was unable to enact her own situations and so was asked to play the role of her mother, who operated a boarding house. In this role she was at ease and seemed to enjoy going on the stage. During the third session the protagonist brought up the fact that one of her roomers was promiscuous. This story was also her own story. As a young girl her illegitimate pregnancy was followed by an abortion, and as she approached middle life she worried about this incident and felt sure her family would find out and would no longer love her. Psychodrama gave this women an opportunity to freely express her feelings about the incident, and the discussion of the audience helped her to see that she had the love of her family and would not necessarily lose it because of that past event.

In the *symbolic distance technique* the protagonist enacts a role very different from his own role and is gradually led to portray his own role. This technique is particularly valuable when working with children. A young boy and girl from broken and inadequate homes were treated in this way. Individual therapy was helpful and outward behavior improved, but the children were afraid to leave the security of the hospital, for they felt sure they could not get along in a home situation. Because the problems of these children were so alike, they were cast as brother and sister and were treated together. Following the portrayals, the group discussed why the children acted differently in the various situations. From these scenes the children finally came to realize that they could get along in some types of family homes and expressed willingness to accept a family care situation.

If the protagonist tends to speak in terms of abstractions, these concepts can be made concrete by symbolizing them as figures with their own personalities: "They"; "society"; "other people"; "the establishment"; "young people"; all can be portrayed by an auxiliary ego. "This woman *is* the Establishment. Talk to her now." The protagonist is directed to confront the auxiliary and eventually role-reverse with her, all of which brings the protagonist's conflicts into sharper focus.

FOCUSING ON THE NONVERBAL

One of the most useful approaches in clarifying the protagonist's problem is the emphasis on explicitly portraying the nonverbal communication involved, e.g.:

JOE: (protagonist) But Sir, you *said* you would.
DIRECTOR: Joe, step out of the scene. Mark, replay that interaction, acting the exact way Joe behaves *(mirror technique)*.

The director asks Mark to shift out of the role of double and to take the role of the *mirror*. (Note: Any person participating in the enactment, except the director and protagonist, is designated by the general term "auxiliary ego".)

MARK: (Auxiliary ego, whining as in Figure 15.) "But Sir, etc. . . .
JOE: Wow! Do I whine like that?

Mirror Technique

FIGURE 15

DIRECTOR: (to group) Is Mark's presentation fair? (Group agrees.) Well,
           Joe . . . with whom did you "whine" as a child? . . .
JOE: To my father . . . when he, etc.

Often what is said in an interaction (the content) is less important than *how* it is said (the process). The dramatization of the expression, posture, tone of voice, angle of the body, and gesture all help bring out the factors that may have been the major determinants of the other person's reaction.

Role reversal, observations from the audience, and the amplification of gesture, as well as the mirror technique, help the protagonist and group become more aware of the nature and importance of the nonverbal communication being portrayed in the interaction.

EXPLORING UNEXPRESSED EMOTIONS

In psychodrama the protagonist presents not only what happened in reality, but more importantly, what may never have actually occurred except in his own fantasy. Moreno has given a term to describe this realm: *surplus reality*. One main importance of psychodrama is that it brings onto the stage the protagonist's hopes, fears, expectations, unexpressed resentments, projections, internalizations, and judgmental attitudes. Furthermore, the protagonist is helped to ventilate these feelings and symbolically live through them.

In the case of the example being used in this chapter, Joe's muted conversation with the boss is converted into an emotional confrontation with the help of the expressive double.

As the scenes are changed to deal with other authority conflicts, a variety of techniques can be used to intensify the expression of feelings.

In dealing with a parent figure, the auxiliary ego as parent stands on a chair, so that Joe feels at a disadvantage. Con-

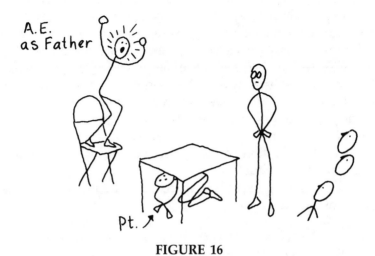

FIGURE 16

versely, Joe may stand on the chair in order to equalize the status and encourage self-assertion (Figure 16).

Colored lights, physical pushing or patronizing "head patting," and increasingly volatile counterconfrontation from the auxiliary can help the protagonist to express the many dimensions of his mixed feelings. In most psychodramas about an authority conflict, not only resentment toward authority is provoked; the need for "a good father" is also tapped.

Moreno calls psychodrama "the theater of truth" because what is enacted is, for the protagonist, the most important truth—the range of his own psychological realities.

MOVING WITH THE RESISTANCES

One major challenge of psychotherapy or psychodrama is that of helping the protagonist find a way to examine those inner feelings that are threatening to his sense of mastery or self-esteem. He may employ a wide range of resistances in order to avoid facing these unpleasant experiences. I find that if the director works *with* the resistances, there can often be a way found to gradually explore the deeper conflicts. Moreno puts it this way: "We don't tear down the protagonist's walls; rather, we simply try some of the handles on the many doors, and see which one opens."

The first step in dealing with a protagonist's resistances is the clear identification and expression of the *manner* in which he is avoiding a situation.

For example, Joe stands transfixed as he begins to think about his father.

DOUBLE: This is very hard for me. I'm not sure I want to talk about this.
JOE: Yes, I feel very tense . . . (The director then has the opportunity to support Joe in his fear.)
DIRECTOR: Being honest with someone so close is difficult—here, in psychodrama, we can face the challenge and it involves taking a risk, but it won't be overwhelming.

The second step in dealing with the resistance is that of exaggerating in the use of the defense. The resistance expressed in the tendency to "explain" may be portrayed openly by the director's asking the protagonist to talk to the group, to *explain* his position for one minute.

The protagonist's statement," "I can't seem to . . ." may be agreed with, but subtly re-defined by the double or the director as, "I won't. . . ."

"I don't know," can be reshaped as, "I don't want to think about that. . . ."

"Why do I have to do this?" can be restated as, "I don't like doing this. . . ."

"It's no use," may be supported, with the addition of the temporary nature of the present resistance. *"Right now* I see no way out. . . ."

The point of going *with* the resistances is that through the explicit portrayal of the defenses, the protagonist becomes more fully aware that he is *choosing* to use a defense, that is, it increases his awareness of his own responsibility for his behavior and sense of mastery over his habitual behavior patterns. The more a protagonist can allow himself, with the support of the director, to say "no," the sooner he begins to feel free to say "yes" when he is ready.

With a protagonist who is becoming overly anxious while dealing with a problem it is often appropriate to allow him to move away from the core conflict, to obtain some "distance." The move from peripheral issues toward central issues described earlier can be temporarily reversed.

A major block in many protagonists is use of the defense mechanism of isolation of affect—they are not even aware that they *are* feeling. The first step in dealing with this resistance is to help the protagonist become aware of the experience of emotion within himself. Secondly, only when he is moved toward an attempt to identify the *quality* of the feeling can he go on to explore the *meaning* of his emotions.

In dealing with sensitizing a protagonist to his own feelings, the director focuses on the protagonist's *nonverbal communications* and his *imagery*. These two "avenues to the unconscious" bypass the most common forms of resistance: intellectualization, vagueness, explanation, rationalization, abstraction, and circumstantiality.

The protagonist's nonverbal communication is dramatized by treating the parts of the protagonist as if they were active beings in themselves: areas of tension in the body, tightness of the voice, gripping of the hands all can be enacted as a little encounter between different parts of the self, e.g.,:

JOE: (to his "father") Daddy, why don't you . . .
DIRECTOR: Joe, what is your voice doing?
JOE: It's choked.

DIRECTOR: Now become the part that's strangling the throat!
   JOE: (as throat) I'm being squeezed and strangled.
DIRECTOR: Now become the part that's strangling the throat!
   JOE: (as strangler, rasping) Shut up, you S.O.B., or you'll get us all into trouble! (as he twists his hands in a wringing motion).

This approach, like dream work, is used in Gestalt therapy and psychosynthesis. Working with dreams can be an important approach for healing (Leutz, 1986; Nolte et al., 1977). This method utilizes the power of metaphor generated by the protagonist's unconscious symbolizing ability.

The use of the *imagery* is a further avenue to the identification of deeper feelings. The different figures in a nightmare, hallucination, or a guided fantasy can interact using psychodramatic methods, and this can often clarify the nature of the protagonist's internal complexes, that is, the conglomerations of attitudes, images, and emotions.

Dealing with a protagonist's resistances is the core of psychotherapy or psychodrama. The "art" of the director is tested nowhere more than in this task. This section of the chapter has only indicated some of the avenues of approach to a challenge that demands an individual response in each situation.

PRESENTING THE BASIC ATTITUDES

An important step in the psychodramatic exploration of a problem is the explicit portrayal of the protagonist's attitudes and basic assumptions about himself, others, and the nature of human relationships. These attitudes are often phrased in terms of internalized sentences, which start with "should" and "ought." Encouraging the protagonist to make these statements explicit is necessary because they represent the values of his superego.

JOE:	(soliloquizing on stage with his double) How could I hate my father? You're not supposed to hate your father!
JOE'S DOUBLE:	Right! I shouldn't hate him no matter what!
JOE:	And anyway, I *love* him! How could I hate him?
DOUBLE:	I can't love and hate at the same time!
JOE:	Well, maybe I can . . .

Not only the protagonist's feelings are to be expressed, but also the attitudes that forbid the feelings from being accepted as part of his self-system. Some of these common attitudes include:

Men aren't supposed to cry
I should be able to handle this myself
Being emotional is a sign of weakness
If I start crying I may never stop
If I express my anger I'm afraid I might lose control or kill someone
If I try to love someone, he should be happy
If I'm not happy, it's because they don't *really* love me
People should be able to resolve their conflicts
I should have known this by now
If I haven't lived up to my expectations, I *must* be a failure

There are hundreds of such "internal commands." Many of these "lies we live by" can be found in the writings of Ronald Laing (1970), Albert Ellis (1962), Walter O'Connell (1963), and many others.

Another way to portray the different attitudes and complexes is to split the protagonist into different "selves," for example, one part might be the judging, rule-pronouncing complex, while the other part is the rebellious, or passive-aggressive, sulking self. This is similar to Fritz Perls' (1969) concept of *top dog vs. underdog*, or Eric Berne's terminology of *Parent, Adult, and Child* (Naar, 1977).

EXPLORING THE CORE CONFLICTS

The problem originally presented is often not at the root of the protagonist's emotional concerns. Basic attitudes have been established in earlier life, and it is the relationships of that period that are the next to be enacted. Sometimes what is indicated is not a movement from the present to the past, but from a relatively superficial to a more personal conflict, such as a sexual problem with a spouse or a struggle between different needs within the protagonist himself.

As these core relationships are portrayed, it may seem obvious to the director or the group that the protagonist is distorting the feelings of the other persons in his life. The director should be in no hurry to correct these distortions. First, the protagonist must present the situation as he experiences it: this is *his* truth. He must experience being listened to. Only then does he become more receptive to exploring the possibility that the situation might have other points of view.

In our example of Joe, the director may explore scenes in which Joe wanted to be accepted by a father who had unrealistically high expectations of him. Joe's fantasies can be portrayed in scenes in which he is abandoned, rejected, or judged as inadequate by his father. Exaggerating the physical relationships may help in clarifying the protagonist's experience of significant events (Figure 17).

Joe role-reverses and portrays his own conception of his father's behavior. Indeed, Joe's portrayal of the father's judgment may be so harsh as to seem unrealistic to the audience, as if Joe is caricaturizing what a "bad father" does. This is probably because he is projecting onto his father the anger and guilt he feels within himself toward the weaknesses that only he himself secretly knows and condemns. Thus, through role reversal the protagonist is helped to portray the distortions of his interpersonal perceptions by acting out

FIGURE 17

what he believes others think (i.e., his own projections). This kind of approach can thus be an effective form of diagnosis of the protagonist's psychodynamics.

ACT HUNGER

Act hunger is the drive toward a fulfillment of the desires and impulses at the core of the self. The director should help the protagonist in a symbolic fulfillment of his act hunger. This is also a fundamental part of the protagonist's "psychological truth."

In the example of the enactment we have been using, the protagonist, Joe, finally confronts his father; he may gain some insight into the rage he has held toward his father by the director's helping him to portray his anger in *act fulfillment*. As the protagonist portrays the anger, themes of need and frustration, which are the bases of the anger, should be interwoven.

It is important that the director be aware of the psy-

FIGURE 18

chotherapeutic maxim, "Don't ventilate the hostility without the protagonist's also experiencing his dependency," that is to say, deal with the protagonist's *need* for something that is frustrated by the significant other. The catharsis of rage is usually a catharsis of longing (Blatner, 1985a).

For example, as Joe confronts his rigid, demanding father, whose unshakable coldness is dramatized and exaggerated by an auxiliary ego, Joe "escalates" his efforts to "get across to the old man," without any success. Finally, he is ready for violence; the director throws him a pillow and says, "There's your father—what do you feel like doing to him?"

Joe begins to beat the pillow, curse at the father, and, with the help of the double and director, express his pent up frustrations:

JOE: You never cared about *me!* All you saw was what *you* wanted! (He continues to strike the pillow, and is beginning to cry) You bastard! I wish you were dead! (Beats the pillow furiously and cries.) (See Figure 18).

At this point, after a full expression, the director may move in several directions. He may bring onto the stage an auxiliary to be the "good father" who can "see Joe for what he really is." The auxiliary may hold Joe and talk to him.

Another very powerful technique is the "death scene." It

can be applied either to the death of the protagonist himself or as a vehicle to review the feelings in relationship to a significant other person (Siroka & Schloss, 1968).

In the first form, the protagonist is instructed to visualize his own death (the director may dim the lights). The director may warm up to the situation by asking him how he died, what it felt like, who is around him, and other related questions. The questions and final statements to others and (through role reversal) of others toward the "dead" protagonist help clarify some of the emotional issues (Rowan, 1973). (This method is useful for emphasizing the role of the "choosing, responsible self";—the "adult" ego state in transactional analysis terms.) Finally, the death scene can move toward a "rebirth scene."

The "death scene" may be interwoven with "judgment scenes," judgment of others, or of the self (Sacks, 1965). The encounter with St. Peter is often a useful technique. (St. Peter is the archetypal figure guarding the gates of heaven who reviews the values and meaning of the protagonist's life with him.) St. Peter can play the role of the friendly and gentle interrogator. If the situation seems more appropriate for a judgment of the protagonist's life, members of the audience can be called in as jurors.

One variation of the death scene I like to use is the shift in St. Peter's role from "judge" to "philosopher." This usually surprises people, for they are expecting St. Peter to be impressed by status and "righteousness" issues, and upset by pecadilloes. Instead, St. Peter simply asks: "How was it?" He does not respond to answers of status, that is, "what the protagonist proved." Rather, he reiterates the focus on the issue of: "Did you do what you had to do? Did you do it in your own way? Did you 'create' along the lines of your natural strengths, inclincations; or did you fulfill your life in a role which was alien to your soul, because you were trying to live up to someone else's expectations?"

Sometimes I follow this scene by giving the protagonist an opportunity to enact the role he would choose if he could be reborn in any kind of life he wanted.

A second major format of the death scene is more commonly used, and involves the death of the significant other person. As the protagonist seems involved in continuously struggling to change the other person, to "make him see," the director may stop and say, "He's dead now. . . ." or, "You have just received a telegram notifying you of his death . . . you rush back and stand at his bedside." Another variation is for the director to say to the protagonist, "You have five minutes to talk to him before he dies. Now is the time to make your goodbyes, ask your final questions, express your honest resentments and appreciations." For example:

> JOE: (to "dying father") Y'know, Dad, I resented your judgment of me as a child. . . .
>
> DIRECTOR: Change parts. (Joe moves over to the empty chair, becoming the father)
>
> JOE: (as father) Well, son, I wanted so much for you . . . but you've done okay. (Change parts)
>
> JOE: Dad . . . how do you feel about me now? (Change parts)
>
> FATHER: Joe . . . I'm kinda proud of you . . . I really am. . . .
>
> JOE: Dad . . . I love you, you know that?
>
> A.E.: (as father) I know, son (Joe weeps.)

Often the son makes his peace with his father in an atonement (at-one-ment). "Saying goodbye" is an important method also for reinforcing the protagonist's sense of identity (Blatner, 1985b; Kaminsky, 1981; Tobin, 1971). "I'm going on . . . I don't need your support any longer . . . I can say goodbye . . . It hurts, but I can let go."

An important principle of healing is that the protagonist, with the help of surplus reality, is enabled to create the desired experience. The technique of "the reformed auxiliary ego" (Sacks, 1970) functions to bring into consciousness the person's needs that have been repressed. In the spirit of what the psychoanalyst Franz Alexander called "an emotionally re-educative experience,": this technique symbolically gratifies that need with the validation of the director and the group. An example of this is a scene in which the auxiliary, having played a rejecting or withholding role in a previous enactment, now is directed to play a more nurturing, positive role (Greenberg-Edelstein, 1986).

Another powerful technique that can sometimes follow a death-and-rebirth scene is "the crib scene." This method is also useful in allowing the protagonist to experience his own dependency needs. The technique is often applied to the entire group, including the protagonist. Doris Twitchell Allen (1966) describes it as follows:

"Today we can be babies—just young infants in a crib. And we can lie on the floor like babies . . . pretend that you are a baby."

Thus, the director gets one after another participant to lie on the floor. After all are on the floor, lying as babies in a crib, the psychodramatic director, in the role of the nurturing mother, walks around from one to the other, patting them and covering them with an imaginary blanket:

"So the baby goes to sleep, warm and quiet. So the baby gets heavy, and goes to sleep . . . And the mother comes and loves the baby. Takes care of the baby. Covers the baby and keeps it warm. Feeds the baby and gives it milk. Pats the baby. Watches over the baby and loves the baby. While the baby sleeps and sleeps." (This is usually repeated several times during a 5-to-20 minute sleep.)

The sleep period is followed by the waking-up period:

"So the baby begins to wake up. Begins to move a little, stretches a little. Opens its eyes. Begins to sit up. Feels good, feels alert, feels happy and content, sits up, gets up, gets back in the chairs."

This is repeated as often as necessary for the group to wake up, and finally ending with:

"Now as you sit back in your chairs you are adults again, acting like adults. But for a while you were a baby and the mother came and loved the baby and took care of the baby."

Back in the chairs, the patients discuss how they felt when they were babies.

Of course, the above-mentioned techniques can be applied in a multiplicity of situations, all depending on the sensitivity of the director.

Act hunger involves more than the expressions of anger and dependency: The protagonist can gain important insights through fulfilling the desire to boast, perform, demand attention, express tenderness, dance, soar, hug, wrestle playfully, fall effortlessly, and so forth. Scenes of act completion can involve death and rebirth, risking and trusting.

Act completion has value in that it validates the protagonist's emotional experiences, thus reinforcing an integration of the previously rejected and suppressed dimensions of the personality—as some protagonists say after a catharsis, "It's OK for me to cry—it doesn't prove I'm weak," or "Wow, I didn't know I had all that anger in me—I thought if I would start to let it out I'd never stop, but I guess I have more self-control than I thought." Thus, the protagonist can accept the anger, dependence, and other negatively valued emotions as part of himself and can redefine himself as one who, as a vital living being, contains many different feelings (Blatner, 1985a; Kellerman, 1984).

Act completion further validates the sense of *active choosing* as part of the self. There are many people who experience life as "happening" to them. They take a passive attitude and feel themselves as rather lifeless and empty inside. The catharsis that so often accompanies the psychodramatic process represents an active taking into the conscious self all the different mixed feelings that had heretofore been rejected and suppressed. Along with the feelings of anger and yearning, there is a sense of "determination to go on," which becomes integrated into the progatonist's self-concept and in turn adds a great deal of vitality to the sense of self.

It should further be noted that the excesses of emotion expressed within a psychodramatic enactment are not likely to lend to a complete loss of control. The presence of the director and group and the expectation of staying within limits act as influences to sustain a small amount of "observing ego" and "controlling ego" in the protagonist's personality. It is rare that a protagonist may begin to extend his destructiveness and stop "pulling his punches," and even then an experienced director can quickly regain control.

SURPLUS REALITY AND ROLE REVERSAL

Following the portrayal of many of the protagonist's fantasies, attitudes, and the fulfillment of act hunger, the protagonist has usually achieved a measure of insight into the nature of his own feelings. To this is now added an exploration of some of the other emotional dimensions of the situation.

For example, the adolescent who has explored some of his own conflicts about taking responsibility (and his externalizations of this conflict onto authority figures) may then portray his future. This is the use of *surplus reality,* the dimensions of alternative past, present, and future events that are a "reality" in the imagination, if not in the outside world (Moreno, 1965). In the *future projection technique,* the adolescent can enact his life five years in the future (Yablonsky, 1954). The protagonist may discover that, as George

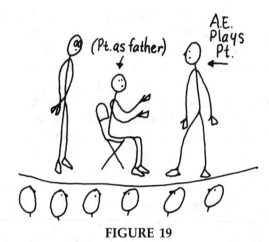

FIGURE 19

Bernard Shaw once said, "There is only one thing worse than not getting what you want—and that is getting what you want!" Through future projection the protagonist can gain a more realistic approach, and begin to portray scenes in which he *can* achieve some successes based on his own work.

Another major form of utilizing surplus reality is to invite the protagonist to put himself in the place of the others in his life (role reversal). Through reversing roles (or changing parts) with the important figures in his psychodrama, the protagonist can develop some important practical and emotional insights into the others' situations. Thus, role reversal becomes a major technique for building the capacity for empathy with others (Figure 19).

For example, in the psychodrama of Joe, the director may have the protagonist explore some of the others' feelings after his catharsis:

DIRECTOR: Now, be your father . . .
    JOE: (as father) All right, I *admit* I did want you to be a football player, 'cause I never had the chance.

DIRECTOR: Change parts.

JOE: (less whining) Well, Dad, that was your dream. I have my own interests—I'm not going to make excuses for myself anymore.

Later, the director may have Joe experience his employer's situation, and in the reversed role position Joe considers the possibility that Mr. Jones is susceptible to pressures from his other subordinates, Joe's co-workers:

JOE: (as Boss) Look, Joe, I really don't like being in this position . . .

Then Joe can be helped to creatively find some approaches that might support his boss and yet help his own position, a way of self-assertion in making tactful constructive suggestions.

In addition, to the use of surplus reality and role reversal, the process of working through, or integration, involves behavioral practice, role training, sharing, discussion, and supportive closure. These dimensions and techniques will be discussed in the next chapter.

SUMMARY

The progress of a psychodrama can be visualized as following the pattern of a curve (Figure 20), as described by Carl Hollander (1978).

The implications of this construction are these:

As the protagonist approaches an apex of feeling, the resistances increase. He is always free to choose or refuse to explore further. This is established at the outset. As resistances grow, the director must continuously work mutually with the protagonist and decide whether to allow for some distance, take an alternative route and work again another day, or attempt to work through the resistances and reach

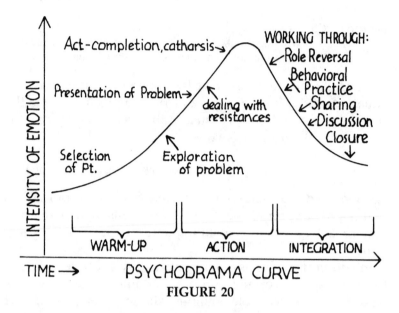

FIGURE 20

the point of emotional openness. (There are many sessions in which the protagonist is not ready to finish his exploration—"working sessions." There is no need for the director to feel that he must produce a dramatic catharsis in each enactment. This only leads to an undue "pushing" of the protagonist, instead of allowing him to grow at his own pace.)

Once the protagonist has reached a point of act completion, catharsis, or otherwise has seemed to achieve his peak of emotion, the director should allow him to move toward *less* emotional intensity (i.e., integration and closure). It becomes confusing if a protagonist attempts to follow one exploration with another. Usually he has enough energy to deal with only one dimension of his life experience in any one session.

In summary, during the enactment, the protagonist is helped toward the gradual portrayal and exploration of the many dimensions of his life. The director attends to the protagonist's progress (1) from dealing with peripheral to dealing with central issues; (2) to portrayal of the spectrum of the protagonist's inner realities (for which reason psychodrama is called "the theater of truth"); (3) toward fulfillment of act hunger in act completion; (4) to the explicit presentation of internal attitudes and feelings, and their integration in "action insight"; (5) to possibly reaching a catharsis; and, finally, (6) to the beginning of exploration of the worlds of the others in the protagonist's "social atom" through role reversal. In the next chapter, the *working through* of these insights will be discussed.

REFERENCES

Allen, D. T. (1954). Psychodrama in the family. *Group Psychotherapy*, 7(1–2), 167–177.

Allen, D. T. (1966). Psychodrama in the crib. *Group Psychotherapy*, 19(1–2), 23–28.

Blatner, A. (1985a). The dynamics of catharsis. *Journal of Group Psychotherapy, Psychodrama & Sociometry*, 37(4), 157–166.

Blatner, A. (1985b). The principles of grief work. In *Creating your living: Applications of psychodramatic methods in everyday life* (pp. 61–72). San Marcos,, TX: Author

Ellis, A. (1962). *Reason and emotion in psychotherapy*. New York: Lyle Stuart.

Greenberg-Edelstein, R. (1986). *The nurturance phenomenon*. Norwalk, CT: Appleton-Century-Crofts.

Hollander, C. (1978). *A process for psychodrama training: The Hollander psychodrama curve*. Denver, CO: Snow Lion Press.

Kaminsky, R. C. (1981). Saying good-by, an example of using a 'good-by' technique and concomitant psychodrama in the resolving of family grief. *Journal of Group Psychotherapy, Psychodrama, & Sociometry*, 34, 100–111.

Kellerman, P. F. (1984). The place of catharsis in psychodrama. *Journal of Group Psychotherapy, Psychodrama & Sociometry*, 37(1), 1–13.

Laing, R. D. (1970). *Knots*. New York: Pantheon Books.

Leutz, G. A. (1986.) The psychodramatic treatment of dreams. *Group Analysis*, 19, 139–146.

Moreno, J. L. (1965). Therapeutic vehicles and the concept of surplus reality. *Group Psychotherapy, 18,* 211–216.

Naar, R. (1977). A psychodramatic intervention within a TA framework in individuals and group psychotherapy. *Group Psychotherapy, Psychodrama & Sociometry, 30,* 127–134.

Nolte, J., Weistart, J., & Wyatt, J. (1977). The psychodramatic production of dreams. *Group Psychotherapy, Psychodrama & Sociometry, 30,* 37–48.

O'Connell, W. (May, 1963). Adlerian psychodrama with schizophrenics. *Journal of Individual Psychology, 19,* 69–76.

Parrish, M. (1953). Psychodrama, description of application and reviews of technique. *Group Psychotherapy, 6*(1–2), 74–77.

Perls, F. (1969). *Gestalt therapy verbatim.* Lafayette, CA: Real People Press.

Rowan, P. J., Jr. (1973). Psychodramatic treatment of death fantasies in adolescent girls. *Handbook of International Sociometry, 7,* 94–98.

Sacks, J. M. (1965). The judgment technique in psychodrama. *Group Psychotherapy, 18*(1–2), 69–72.

Sacks, J. M. (1970). The reformed auxiliary ego technique: A psychodramatic rekindling of hope. *Group Psychotherapy, 23,* 118–126.

Schulman, B. (1960). A psychodramatically oriented action technique in group psychotherapy. *Group Psychotherapy, 13*(1–2), 34–38.

Siroka, R. & Schloss, G. (1968). The death scene in psychodrama. *Group Psychotherapy, 21*(4), 202–205.

Tobin, S. A. (1971). Saying goodbye in Gestalt therapy. *Psychotherapy: Theory, Research and practice, 8*(2), 150–155.

Yablonsky, L. (1954). The future-projection technique. *Group Psychotherapy, 7*(3–4), 303–305.

6

Working Through: Behavioral Practice, Sharing, and Closing

The third and last phase of psychodramatic enactment, following the warm-up and action portions, is the time for *working through*. The protagonist is ready to restore his general equilibrium by (1) developing some sense of mastery over his problem, (2) receiving group support while reconstituting his defenses, and (3) dealing with issues of reparation and "reentry" into the outside world.

The challenge of mastery in working through may be one of the major tasks of the enactment. By mastery, I refer to the development of effective behavioral responses to a stressful situation. What approach would be the best in asking the boss for a raise? How can the protagonist communicate with his father using some of his new insights when he returns home for a holiday visit? What should the protagonist say to a friend who seems to want things "his way" all the time?

In psychodrama, the protagonist is helped to integrate the dimensions of his nonrational feelings into the decisions that concern these tasks. Ventilation, exploration, association, and catharsis may all be part of that process (as discussed in the previous chapter). However, in some settings (such as school or work) where personal disclosure is not appropriate, the task of finding better behavioral responses may nevertheless be approached through the media of *role playing, sociodrama,* or *role training* (see Chapter 1). In these approaches, much of the personal exploration that was discussed in the previous chapter is not necessary. The working through portion occupies the major portion of the session's time and consists primarily of *behavioral practice.*

In this chapter, I will discuss the techniques involved in behavioral practice, sharing, and closing.

BEHAVIORAL PRACTICE

The function of behavioral practice is to experiment with a variety of new behaviors (1) in a "fail-safe" context, (2) with feedback regarding the effectiveness of these trial behaviors, and (3) with opportunities for repeated attempts until some degree of satisfaction is achieved. These three components are invaluable in the protagonist's working through of his problem. The behavioral practice may or may not be associated with a deeper level of emotional exploration.

TECHNIQUES OF BEHAVIORAL PRACTICE

The first step in behavioral practice is setting up the enactment in the same way as described in the warm-up and the first part of the chapter on action. Once the situation is presented and the protagonist and auxiliary egos are involved in the scene, the director proceeds to get feedback on the protagonist's behavior.

The protagonist may simply be asked how he feels about his response and how he might like to try it differently. Members of the group may also be asked for their observations and/or suggestions. Furthermore, group members may be invited to show how they would handle the situation in the enactment:

1. The protagonist role reverses and replays the scene, thus experiencing the situation from the other person's point of view. The auxiliary ego is instructed to act in the same way as the protagonist behaved, and thus the protagonist learns what it is like to be on the receiving end of his own behavior.

2. An auxiliary ego portrays the behavior of the protagonist, who steps out of the scene and observes. This is one form of the *mirror technique*. Group consensus is sought by the director to assure that the auxiliary ego's behavior is a fairly accurate portrayal of the protagonist's nonverbal style. If the group feels that the auxiliary ego is inaccurate, he is either given another chance to replay the scene and correct his behavior, or someone else can enact the scene as he saw it happen. Finally, the protagonist can reenter the scene and try again. In many ways this is similar to the use of videotape in group psychotherapy.

After the protagonist receives feedback as to how he had been behaving, and some possible ideas as to how he might act differently, the director encourages him to repeatedly replay the scene until he finds a response that fits his own temperament and meets the requirements of the situation to his own satisfaction.

For the protagonist who has difficulty creating a different response, the director can suggest that he try a behavior that would be "the worst possible response." Alternatively, the protagonist might be asked to behave in a way that would be totally different from his habitual style. Specifically, the protagonist may be directed to play the scene being silly, brutally frank, very cautious and indirect, or confrontational. Experimenting with these artificial manners gives the protagonist freedom to take a risk (because he was *told* to act that way) and to perhaps find that there are aspects of his new behavior that he might wish to integrate into his own style. For example, in a group setting, two of the participants in a nonverbal exercise interacted in a very constricted fashion. After some discussion, the two people were asked to repeat the exercise in a way in which they would never behave in their everyday lives. They proceeded to interact in a silly, awkward, rough-and-tumble manner. Afterwards, they reported feeling foolish, but admitted that they enjoyed themselves tremendously. To their surprise, the group reinforced their risk-taking by responding that they were delighted with the two persons' spontaneity.

Another approach to behavioral practice is for the director to suggest *specific* behaviors in the enactment, for example, "Try asserting yourself while you stand with your pelvis tilted forward and your jaw thrust out"; "Answer your mother with the palms of your hands facing downwards instead of turned upwards in a pleading gesture."

It should be emphasized again that in psychodramatic enactments in which the protagonist's *self-understanding* is the major task, it is best to deal with issues of working through and behavioral practice only *after* the protagonist has first ventilated and explored the *meaning* of his emotions. Moreno notes: "Enactment comes first, retraining comes later. We must give [the protagonist] the satisfaction of act completion first, before considering retraining for behavioral changes."

APPLICATIONS OF BEHAVIORAL PRACTICE

There are several subtypes of behavioral practice:

Professional skills training. Skills in interviewing, history-taking, counseling, or giving support can all be developed with role-playing: What should one say to a dying patient? How does one ask about sexual issues in interviewing? What is the best response to an irritated or dissatisfied customer?

Assertion training. This is a major area of behavior therapy in clinical psychology: How should one stand up to a dominating friend or resist peer pressures? How can one say "no" to a persistent salesman? How does one ask for a date? (this takes self-assertion); What is the best way to speak up at a meeting? (Powell, 1985).

These methods can be used to help shy, constricted people become more forceful. In addition, behavioral practice can help histrionic, overly dramatic personalities to be less forceful or to develop more matter-of-fact and appropriate styles of relating.

Desensitization. For those who tend to become easily flustered or frightened, repeated reenactments of an anxiety-provoking situation in a supportive setting can reduce the avoidance response. In this context, behavioral practice is an action approach similar in spirit to Wolpe's "reciprocal inhibition" and other "deconditioning" approaches for phobias, impotence, and other psychological problems. Examples include enacting the response to being frightened by a spider, or building gradual step-wise reactions to a sexually provocative situation.

Role-training. Related to the above-mentioned approaches, some groups can be helped with challenges of role transitions; chronically institutionalized psychiatric patients can be prepared for leaving the hospital by practicing situations of seeking employment, returning home, and even simple tasks such as opening a bank account or going on an airplane; parents-to-be can practice simulated bathing of the baby; a teenager who has recently had a colostomy can prepare for embarrassing questions from schoolmates; parents can explore different approaches to the management of behavior problems in their children.

Spontaneity training. The last major subtype of behavioral practice is the experimentation with *play* modalities. Many people have forgotten how to allow themselves to be spontaneous and playful (Blatner & Blatner, 1988). Opportunities to expand the imagined range of possible roles can extend the protagonist's sense of mastery over a variety of situations, for example, playing roles of the hero, villain, tyrant, newborn baby, animal, tree, God, seductress, prima donna, and so on. (See Chapter 9 on theory for more discussion of the place of spontaniety training.)

Thus behavioral practice in its many forms can serve as an invaluable aid in working through a problem. Trial behaviors are explored in a "fail-safe" context, and support and reinforcements are given to more appropriate responses.

SHARING

Once the protagonist has finished his enactment, he is in the process of becoming gradually more reflective, less warmed-up, and is ready to receive some feedback. In the enactment, his physical involvement and spontaneity have rendered him very vulnerable to the judgments of the others in the group—much more vulnerable than if he had used only his verbal defenses in a narrative form. Instead of permitting a potentially humiliating "analysis," the director uses the psychodramatic technique of *sharing*. In sharing, the director seeks feedback that puts a premium on support and on the self-disclosure of the group members (Barbour, 1972, 1977; Pitzele, 1980).

THE TECHNIQUE OF SHARING

The director and the protagonist sit down together to begin the interaction with the group. The spontaneous feelings of closeness or the intuitive sense of the protagonist's needs determine how close people are to sit and whether body touching is appropriate.

Psychodramas that have produced a catharsis or a portrayal of a very moving situation sometimes close with hugging and shared crying among the group members and the protagonist. Other enactments in which the protagonist has made a "breakthrough" using the media of playfulness may close with triumphal activity. The primary guidelines for the director are based on the spontaneous, genuine feelings of the people involved, rather than the applications of any superficial technique.

I discourage the ritualistic practice of applause after a psychodramatic enactment: I think it cheapens the whole process. (This is to be differentiated from an allowable spontaneous burst of joyous applause when something happens during an enactment that evokes the group's enthusiasm.)

Once the protagonist is seated, the director explains *sharing* to the group:

Now is the time for sharing. The protagonist (use his name, e.g., "Joe") has shared with you a very personal part of his life; he has left himself vulnerable to your comments. Rather than give an "analysis," it would be more appropriate for us to respond authentically and subjectively. How has Joe's drama touched each of you? What have *you* experienced that relates to Joe's situation?"

At this point, several people usually express past or present conflicts in their own lives and share the mixed feelings that they too have felt (Figure 21). The auxiliary egos may also be invited to share the reactions they experienced "in role"—i.e., as the protagonist's father, employer, as well as their own real life feelings.

Some group members tend to opinionate, for example, "I felt you were being really passive with your father and that this is probably due to your relationship with your mother."

FIGURE 21

(A sentence beginning with "I feel" can still be an opinion.) The director should abruptly intervene and reiterate the instructions about sharing: "This is not the time to talk about Joe's problem. How has his story touched *your* life?" If others try to talk about their own feelings, but because of defensive habit, continue to say, "You feel . . ." or "You want . . ." the director may gently remind them to take responsibility for their own statements: "You mean, '*I* feel' " Usually group members will respond quickly and proceed talking about their *own* experiences in the first person.

If no one in the group initiates the sharing, it could be due to several causes: (1) the group is not warmed up enough; (2) the group cohesion is still weak and others are afraid to disclose themselves; (3) the protagonist's enactment was too abstract or the situation too foreign to the group; (4) the protagonist's position was very different from group norms or values; or (5) the group is angry with the protagonist or director. Each situation must be dealt with creatively by the director.

One approach to resistance in the group's sharing is for the director to simply repeat that the protagonist has given each of them a "gift," and that it would be unfair for the group not to share in return.

In another approach, the director says, "Look around at

the group . . . look at their eyes . . . they are telling you their feelings." Or, she can ask the protagonist, "Who do you think is touched by your story?"

Sometimes the group may have a need to share not only with the protagonist, but also with the "person" played by one of the auxiliary egos—such as the protagonist's father: "I really understood what you had to go through, Mr. Smith, because I too have a son like Joe (the protagonist), and I felt the same way . . ." The director asks the group to share with the significant other person in the protagonist's life *after* the group shares with the protagonist. This technique can keep the end of the session in action and may allow for a more complete closure.

Most of the time, the sharing proceeds smoothly. Often the sharing by one of the other group members may lead directly into another psychodrama: "My mother never understood me either; and I rejected her . . . and now she's dead!" (Weeps) The group member who shared now becomes the protagonist and is helped to enter his own enactment (he is already warmed up!). Indeed, a long session may have several psychodramas, each triggered by the other.

It is very important for both group members and the protagonist to have a time of sharing. Not only does this provide mutual support, but misunderstandings that may have arisen during the session can then be clarified through the opportunity for questions and feedback.

For example, in a role-playing session with nursery school teachers, the problem arose as to how to set up a conference with the resistant mother of an aggressive child. Several teachers in turn took the role of the one who was trying to coax, cajole, or firmly instruct the "mother" (played by one of the group members) to make an appointment. Finally, one of the teachers, Mary, risked being "too hard" and set down an ultimatum: "Either the mother comes in by a specified date or the child must leave the school." The teacher playing the mother became furious, and vigorously tongue-lashed Mary for this "unreasonable" position. The group broke into a burst of spontaneous applause. After the role-playing was over, there was no time left for sharing.

In the next session, a week later, Mary reported having experienced anxiety during the interval: She felt the group rejected her because of her stand. Mary felt that the rejection was "proved" by the group's applause at the angry response of the other teacher (as mother). The group was surprised, and vociferously reassured Mary that the applause was not *against* her; indeed, they felt her stance was most effective. The applause was for the *other* teacher's burst of spontaneous, "angry" emotion! It was not that the group agreed with the "mother," but that they were delighted with the other teacher's open *expression of affect*—so hungry were they for some active, emotional interchange. Although Mary was pleased to receive this reassurance, she had still undergone a week of unnecessary worry. The director should have paced herself so that the sharing and feedback occurred right after the enactment.

In summary, the sharing period provides an opportunity for all of the participants in a psychodrama to ventilate their feelings. The group members need this as much as the protagonist does. The catharsis in the drama may then spread, be reexperienced, and subside as the group realizes its common bond of human feelings.

CLOSING

At the end of a group session, the director may wish to finish with a variety of approaches. The length of the session, the degree of cohesion and self-disclosure achieved, and the task of the group are all variables to be considered. Often a period of discussion may follow the sharing, which could lead to a further "winding down" of the level of tension.

Some of the components of closing to be considered include the following:

1. *Dealing with "reentry."* How will the group members adapt what they have learned to their everyday lives? This is especially important after long or otherwise intensive sessions.

2. *Summarizing.* In more task-oriented groups, where personal involvement has been limited, a summary of what has gone on and discussion of implications and plans may be in order.

3. *Planning the next session.* In ongoing therapy groups, future agendas may be discussed. Perhaps one of the group specifically volunteers to be a protagonist, or it is agreed that a certain theme will be dealt with.

4. *Support.* If one protagonist has become particularly vulnerable due to his participation and risk-taking in an enactment or confrontation, and the director feels he may need some additional support, she may wish to use a specific *ego-building technique,* for example, all of the members in the group tell the protagonist something they like about him.

5. *Unfinished business.* There may yet be a sense of unspoken feelings between group members (including the director). One technique is *resentments and appreciations:* "Before we close, we can ventilate any unfinished business. It's not always necessary to work these things out, but it's important that the unspoken feelings be expressed openly before we end." (The group is drawn into a circle) "You may want to share directly the resentments and/or appreciations you feel for each other. Now is the time to do so." Then the group members speak up as they feel the need: "Nancy, I resent the way you judged me"; "Bill, I appreciate your support, and resent your pity"; and so forth.

6. *Closing rituals.* There are a variety of closing techniques such as simply holding hands in a circle, leading the group in a guided fantasy, etc.

7. *Dealing with separation.* The "intimacy" experienced in groups that have had much emotional exchange is often such a new experience to the group members that they resist letting go of the group cohesion. Ritualizing the separation experience can often be useful, for examaple, the group forms a close circle and each person is instructed to look at the other and say "goodbye" to every other person in the group. (It is not necessary to do this one at a time; all can do it simultaneously.)

SUMMARY

This chapter has discussed the activities of the third and last phases of the psychodramatic enactment. The working through of the problem using behavioral practice may either be a way of following up the insight or may itself dominate the session. Following the enactment, the director moves into the sharing phase, and finally closes, using a variety of techniques.

REFERENCES

Barbour, A. (1972). The self disclosure aspect of the psychodrama sharing session. *Group Psychotherapy and Psychodrama, 25,* 132–138.

Barbour, A. (1977). Variations on psychodramatic sharing. *Group Psychotherapy, Psychodrama & Sociometry, 30,* 122–126.

Blatner, A. & Blatner, A. (1988). *The art of play: An adult's guide to reclaiming imagination and spontaneity.* New York: Human Sciences Press.

Feinberg, H. (1959). The ego building technique. *Group Psychotherapy 12*(3–4), 230–235.

Goldfield, M. (1968). Use of TV videotape to enhance the value of psychodrama. *American Journal of Psychiatry, 125*(5), 690–692.

Heilbrun, G. (1967). On sharing. *American Journal of Psychotherapy, 21*(4), 750.

Kellerman, P. F. (1988). Closure in psychodrama. *Journal of Group Psychotherapy, Psychodrama & Sociometry, 41*(1), 21–29.

Pitzele, M. S. (1980). Moreno's chorus: The audience in psychodrama. *Group Psychotherapy, Psychodrama & Sociometry, 33*, 139–141.

Powell, M. F. (1985). A program of life-skills training through interdisciplinary group processes. *Journal of Group Psychotherapy, Psychodrama & Sociometry, 38*(1), 23–34.

Speros, T. (1972). The final empty chair. *Group Psychotherapy, 25*(1–2), 32–33.

Sturm, I. E. (1965). The behavioristic aspects of psychodrama. *Group Psychotherapy, 18*(1–2), 50–64.

7

Principles and Pitfalls

The effective helping relationship is characterized by certain basic principles, which involve the development of the helper's sense of professional commitment and intellectual humility, as well as forming a truly mutual relationship with clients. These principles apply equally well to the leadership of any group in which human feelings are subject to expression and examination, irrespective of the method used. In the use of psychodrama, many pitfalls are possible whenever the principles that underlie the method are forgotten. In this chapter, I discuss some of these issues more fully.

THE CONTEXT OF MUTUALITY

The principle of mutuality refers to the wholehearted respect of the client as one who is growing and exploring in his own way. Within the group the sense of mutual trust can only grow when based on norms of respect. The director may comment on some of these norms in her introductory remarks:

"During this group session, each of you will be responsible for choosing your own directions. You may proceed at your own pace. You will benefit from these sessions in direct proportion to your own active participation and the extent to which you are willing to take some risks."

"My role is to help you clarify your goals and feelings. I can show you some methods which you may find helpful in redefining your experiences more creatively. More importantly, in this group I will attempt to develop an atmosphere in which you will feel ready to explore."

The purpose of this kind of introduction is to establish a norm of mutual trust and respect. An approach that suggests a confrontational attitude only tends to increase the defensiveness of everyone in the group.

Excessive catalysts are not appropriate in group settings because the process of the group is in itself powerful enough to engender a great deal of motivation for exploration. The use of psychodramatic methods as warm-ups can greatly facilitate this process. The director can also use psychodramatic methods in later stages of the group process, in order to resolve conflicts and clarify issues. "Clever" interpretations and confrontations by the leader are relatively unimportant in the overall growth process.

Not only should the director avoid confrontational attacks, but she should also limit the tendency of group members to subtly attack each other. The practice of giving feedback when it is not asked for is often a form of externalization or projection on the part of the person making the interpretation. The director may identify the source of such thinly veiled attacks by gently saying to the speaker, "You seem genuinely concerned about X's behavior. Would you care to explore what it is about *his* behavior that affects *you* so deeply?"

PROFESSIONAL HUMILITY

It is essential that the director have an awareness of the strengths and limitations of the many methods in helping personal development. Over the last decade, scores of innovations have been introduced into the fields of psychotherapy, education, and management. All too often the proponents of these new methods tend to idealize their pet approach. This leads to the pitfall of applying that method indiscriminately: Those protagonists for whom a certain approach is ineffective may be coerced into useless efforts at staying with that method. The true professional knows that there are many varied populations that require different therapeutic or educational approaches.

PATHOLOGICAL SPONTANEITY

The principle of spontaneity can also be misused. Group leaders often deal with countertransference reactions to a protagonist by getting angry at him, and then rationalize this behavior by calling it "being authentic," "modeling anger," "confrontation," or "feedback." Exhibiting any and all impulses is not the purpose of developing spontaneity. When grossly misused, this kind of expressiveness could be called *pathological spontaneity.*

The attacking behavior described above usually represents a form of acting-out of the director's own countertransference (i.e., the therapist's emotional reaction to her patient). Another form of countertransference behavior is the inappropriate use of undue physical contact, sexual advances, or sarcasm. The motivating forces for these types of behavior are manifold, and the director is cautioned to continuously assess her own behavior to prevent this most prevalent pitfall for all those in the helping role.

One of the most common sources of countertransference behavior arises from the director's need to prove that she is professionally competent by obtaining "results." She thus becomes impatient with the realities of personal growth: its essentially *gradual* nature, fraught with resistances, defenses, and flagging motivation. If the director feels personally threatened, whether consciously or unconsciously, by her protagonist's slow progress or reactions, she is likely to engage in a variety of maneuvers: subtly provoking guilt, generally barraging the protagonist with words in an effort "to get a point across," nagging, and other confrontations. If the director is not aware of her countertransference reactions, she may fall into the major error of pushing and coercing her clients, or allowing other group members to act out her own needs. This is the source of most of the worst abuses prevalent in therapeutic groups and similar settings. A less obvious abuse occurs through a leader's passivity. It is not helpful for a group leader to indulge in excessively nondirective behavior. Important countertransference issues are apparent in this leadership stance also. Many of these reactions happen to even the most experienced therapists, but one must learn to watch out for them and not inflict them on the group.

ACTION VS. AWKWARDNESS

Although the director of a psychodramatic enactment should generally strive to keep the action going, she must nevertheless avoid the pitfall of trying too hard to attain technical virtuosity. It is much better to be awkward than to be clever. A truly polished enactment can be gained from the use of scripts and rehearsals, as is sometimes done in modified forms of creative dramatics—an error, in my opinion, because the use of rehearsed material loses the essential nature of psychodrama—its spontaneity. If spontaneity seems awkward, let it be: the group moves in to "help" the director.

Nevertheless, the director need not be self-consciously hesitant with statements such as, "Why don't you . . .";

"How would you feel about . . ."; "Would you like to . . ." It is better to be gently positive. Once the freedom to say "no" has been clearly established, the director can speak with assurance: "Be your father . . ."; "Show us . . ." "Let's . . ."

PROFESSIONAL CONSIDERATIONS

The director should be aware of the problems in leading different kinds of groups. The principles of working with hospitalized psychiatric patients are quite different from those involved in leading a personal development group. The following issues are only several of the challenges that should be carefully considered by any group leader:

1. *Selection*. The director should be aware of the problems inherent in including certain types of people in a group.
   a. Those who are embroiled in life crisis may dominate the group's attention unless they have someone else from whom they can receive counseling. It is not the purpose of a group session to take *full* responsibility for helping one of its members to make decisions about major life transitions, or to cope with losses. Of course, the group may serve as a useful *adjunct* in such cases.
   b. Those who would likely become disruptive or unusually demanding should be carefully evaluated in the selection process, especially clients who are actively psychotic, depressed, histrionic, or intoxicated with a stimulant at the time of the group meeting.
   c. Those who are attending the group *against* the advice of their therapist risk becoming psychiatric casualties. Another category of persons who are particularly vulnerable to the group process are the alienated and socially isolated who have no network of family or friends to which they return after the group.

d. Those who, against their better judgment, allow themselves to be overtly or covertly coerced into attending the group, for example, those coming as part of an institutional in-service training program; as a requirement of work or at the request of a supervisor or employer; as part of an educational curriculum in order to obtain required credits; or under pressure from family, friends, or other helping persons in the community.

e. Those expecting a level of participation or self-disclosure that is different from the plans or expectations of the group leader or group. The director should see to it that the group knows her plans before they decide whether or not to attend, for example, if she plans to go "deep," or to get into more intimate and personal issues, she should make this clear.

2. *Follow-up.* The director should be in such a position that she can assure that her group members will have access to further psychotherapy if needed. It is advisable for the director to have some psychiatric support—colleagues who can provide medication, hospitalization, or other forms of crisis intervention. Although these forms of follow-up are rarely needed, arranging for this "back-up" reflects the director's professional awareness of the nature of the impact of group process.

3. *Working with systems.* The director may be asked to lead a group of co-workers or students within an organization, for example, a community agency, a business, a school system, and so forth. These situations require an awareness of some pitfalls involved with consultation to systems. It is also advisable for the director to be well-versed in principles of consultation before undertaking the leadership of such a group. Some of the pitfalls include the following:

a. When dealing with co-workers, the director should beware of the personal vulnerability that can be engendered through the use of action techniques. For this reason, it is often better to limit the use of psychodramatic methods to problem-oriented rather than personal-oriented approaches (i.e., using role-playing or sociodrama rather than psychodrama). It is rare that a group of those who live, work, or study together is so cohesive and free of internal competitiveness that it can tolerate the extensive, symmetrical self-disclosure that is required in the use of psychodrama. However, many psychodramatic methods can be adapted to these group situations.

b. The use of physical contact is an especially powerful modality and should be used with the greatest of caution. Among adolescents and other groups, the use of touching and hugging tends to take on a distinctly sexual and/or threatening significance.

c. The group will often subtly manipulate the director into staging a scene dealing with a co-worker (usually a supervisor) who is *not present*. "How do you deal with this person?" is the innocent topic of the role-playing. Actually, the director is being asked to ally against this person as the group works out its externalizations, displacements, and avoidance of self-examination. The director should beware of this trap: The content of the session often backfires when it comes to the attention of the supervisor.

THE CLIENT-CENTERED SPIRIT OF PSYCHODRAMA

Much of what has been described in this chapter reflects an underlying philosophy that is essentially consistent with the spirit of Carl Rogers' "client-centered therapy." It should be noted at the outset that the therapist need not be passive in order to engage mutually with her client. The term "non-directive," which has been used to describe Rogers' approach, refers to the therapist's avoidance of determining the *content* of the interaction. It is quite possible, however, for a therapist to be quite active and directive in helping her client to use a variety of *methods* to *explore* his problem. Thus, as in psychodrama, one can be directive in terms of *process* while still maintaining a true client-centered mutuality.

Rogers' most valuable contribution, in my opinion, has been his noting the essential conditions for an effective helping relationship, whatever the theoretical orientation of the helper. These conditions include: (1) the authenticity of the way the therapist relates to her client; (2) the establishment of a bond of *empathy* between therapist and client; and (3) the therapist's development of a capacity for *positive regard* for her client. I find these principles to be profound, and I learn new facets and levels of these ideas as I continue to pursue the art of psychotherapy. Furthermore, Rogers's ideas are applicable to a variety of educational and psychotherapeutic methodologies, including the use of psychodramatic techniques.

SUMMARY

When psychodramatic methods are used without the proper philosophical foundations, the director is in danger of falling into some common errors. These pitfalls can be avoided if the director applies certain basic principles that allow the protagonist to develop at his own pace, in a context of mutuality, and without aggressive confrontation from the group leader. In short, they follow the conditions of client-centered therapy. The director must also remain aware of such group process issues as problems of selection and follow-up, the tendency to idealize one approach, and the ability of the director to tolerate ambiguity.

REFERENCES

Blank, L. (1971). Confrontation techniques—A two-sided coin. In L. Blank & C. Gottsegen (Eds.) *Confrontation: Encounters in self and interpersonal awareness.* New York: Macmillan.

Fink, A. K. (1963). The democratic essence of psychodrama. *Group Psychotherapy, 16,* 156–160.

Freundlich, D. (1971). A psychoanalytic hypothesis of change mechanisms in encounter groups. *International Journal of Group Psychotherapy, 23*(1), 42–53.

Gazda, G. M. (1975). Some tentative guidelines for ethical practice of group work practitioners. In G. M. Gazda (Ed.), *Basic approaches to group psychotherapy and group counseling* (2nd ed.) (pp. 55–65). Springfield, IL: Charles C Thomas.

Hurewitz, P. (1970). Ethical considerations in leading therapeutic and quasitherapeutic groups: Encounter and sensitivity groups. *Group Psychotherapy, 23*(1–2), 17–20.

Knepler, A. E. (1959). Role playing in education—some problems in its use. *Group Psychotherapy, 12*(1), 32–41.

Kuehn, J. L., & Crinella, F. (1969). Sensitivity training: Interpersonal "overkill" and other problems. *American Journal of Psychiatry, 126*(12), 840–845.

Moreno, J. L. (1957). Code of ethics of group psychotherapists. *Group Psychotherapy, 10,* 143. (This was one of the first articles on the subject.)

Ross, W. D., Kligfeld, M., & Withers, R. (1971). Psychiatrists, patients and sensitivity groups. *Archives of General Psychiatry, 25*(2), 178.

Sandron, L. (1973). Psychodrama with hostile group members. *Handbook of International Sociometry, 7,* 29–36.

Winthrop, H. (1971). Abuses of sensitivity training on American campuses. *Bulletin of Menninger Clinic, 35*(1), 128–141.

Yalom, I. (1985). *Theory and practice of group psychotherapy.* 3rd Edition. New York: Basic Books.

8

Applications of Psychodramatic Methods

Psychodramatic techniques may be effectively used in any field that requires some exploration of the psychological dimensions of a problem. The fields of education, psychotherapy, and industrial relations have discovered that approaches that integrate participatory, experiential learning with verbal and cognitive analysis are the most beneficial for a program that aims at fully involving their clients in mutual explorations of multidimensional problems. This chapter will note some of the major categories of the contexts in which psychodramatic methods are currently being applied. Of course, each director must modify the methodology in order to meet the needs of her own style and ability, as well as the situation of the client and the realities of her helping role.

I. THE MENTAL HEALTH PROFESSIONS

The most common area in which psychodramatic methods are applied is in the field of mental health. In hospitals, clinics, daycare centers, crisis units, alcohol and drug programs, therapeutic communities, and many other settings, many professionals have found a role for psychodramatic methods in their therapeutic range of approaches. Sometimes psychodrama itself is used as a distinct program. More often, methods and techniques derived from psychodrama are integrated into the process of individual, group, and conjoint family therapy.

Group therapy. Enactments of varying lengths may be interspersed with periods of discussion. Action methods (such as those mentioned in the chapter on warm-ups) can often be woven into the ongoing group process. Especially effective are the techniques of doubling, role reversal, or the interjection of an exercise of nonverbal communication. These function to circumvent some of the verbal impasses that occur so often in therapy groups.

For example, at one point in a group session, the members became involved in a series of abstract generalizations about philosophical issues. They seemed to have lost their sense of direction. The conversation was sparse and full of platitudes, and the members were no longer in touch with their own concerns and needs. The director threw a book of matches onto the floor in the middle of the group and told them that this was to be a symbol of something they all wanted, even though they might not be clear on just what that was. They were asked to physically deal with the matchbook, as if it were that valuable "something" they desired. One member picked it up, played with it, then gave it to another. A variety of responses followed: a sequence of giving, grabbing, tearing, holding, offering, and rejecting the book of matches. After a few minutes, the action was stopped; the result was that the group felt it had quite a bit to talk about: why one person used the matches one way, and how another person reacted in a different fashion. The group began to talk about their interactional styles, their associations to the symbol, and their feelings about the way they had dealt with it. (In a different group, when a small object did not receive a quick warm-up, a chair was introduced as the symbol; since it necessitated more work to manipulate a chair, the corresponding increase in physical involvement led to a great deal of group interaction.)

Another group problem is the situation in which a member or a subgroup is dissatisfied or planning to leave the group. The spectrogram is a psychodramatic technique that can be used to clarify the issues and illustrate the feelings of the group: Those feeling one way place themselves toward one side of the room, those feeling a different way go to the other side, and those who are indifferent in the middle (Kole, 1967). This is followed by a discussion about any or all of the subgroups, and it helps to minimize the anxiety of members who feel that they are the only ones in the group who feel the way they do. In groups dealing with a member of a subgroup who wants to leave, the facilitator may use the *behind-your-back* technique. Using this technique, those who wish to leave may symbolically do so by turning their backs, and the rest of the group is instructed to discuss their leaving as if it had actually happened. (It should be noted that the *behind-your-back technique* can be a very powerful and potentially destructive method of confrontation unless used with skill and judgment.) As the group talks, those who have "left the group" may be tempted to reenter the group in order to correct misunderstandings and represent their case. They might also hear that there are others in the group who sympathize with them and defend them, and this too may induce them to return. In either case, the technique offers a shared experience that the group will then be able to discuss with an increased feeling of cohesion.

A third example is illustrated in a therapy group with adolescents. Bill, a young man, was explaining his tendency to joke and be superficial in his relationships with others. He said that he was aware that he was not letting himself become "close." Bill explained that if he were to be rejected after he had allowed himself to really care about another person, he was afraid he would be deeply hurt. He said that

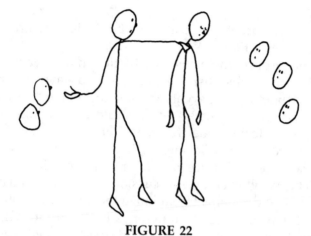

FIGURE 22

he wouldn't be able to stand it. The therapist had Bill recreate the situation and then helped him enact the feelings of one who is rejected, for example, the questions as to his own guilt, the fears of being rejected for something about himself that he couldn't change, and so forth. In facing these issues, Bill learned that being rejected need not result in a catastrophic injury to one's self-esteem; indeed, although he was hurt, he was strong enough not to break down (Figure 22). This sense of inner strength was an enjoyable alternative to Bill's rationalized avoidance of closeness, and was reinforced by the group norm of not having to treat each other with "kid gloves."

In similar ways, this technique can be used to enact threats of loss of control over love, anger, grief and other emotions, as well as other excuses for avoiding goal-directed behavior. The result of these enactments, in which the fear is faced, results in an increasing sense of self-control.

Family Therapy and Marital Counseling. Psychodramatic methods can escalate the interchange to a more authentic level of emotional encounter, which, in turn, facilitates a more productive exploration of the problems in the relationships among the participants.

In some marital couple therapy meetings it becomes apparent that an "adversary system" has been established in the couple's relationship; that is, each partner seems to be trying to "win" by justifying personal actions and blaming the other's behavior. For example, Nancy and Doug seemed to be stuck in complaining about what they *do not* want the other to do or say. In such confrontations, I have utilized the technique of role reversal, directing each person to take the part of the spouse. Then, I address them using the spouse's name and ask them in-role to tell each other, not what they do not want, but rather what they *do* want. If it seems that the person caricaturizes the partner by demanding the obviously impossible, I point this out, and encourage a more realistic portrayal. This approach, I found, has frequently "broken" the mental set in which each partner views the other as "uncaring," "selfish," or "withholding."

II. PSYCHODRAMATIC METHODS WITH CHILDREN AND ADOLESCENTS

Psychodramatic techniques are utilized to help young people explore the emotional conflicts in their lives at all age levels, and in all contexts—in the home, the child-guidance clinic, residential treatment centers, speech and hearing clinics, nursery schools, recreation centers, summer camps, the classroom, and *in-situ* (i.e., on the spot wherever the situation arises), on the playground, or the front yard (Figure 23).

In addition, psychodramatic methods, when modified for the setting, can be remarkably effective for children with relatively poor cognitive and verbal skills—such as the mentally retarded or preadolescent delinquents. Indeed, the use of role-playing techniques is a valuable approach to *building* verbal skills in these action-prone children.

IN SITU:

FIGURE 23

Furthermore, psychodramatic techniques can be integrated with other forms of activity, play, and story-telling therapies.

III. APPLICATIONS IN PRIMARY AND SECONDARY EDUCATION

Psychodramatic methods can be applied in many different school settings. Most of the time, the use of these methods should be limited to role-playing or sociodrama. This is because the more personal explorations that are involved in psychodrama may lead to too much self-disclosure for the protagonist in a context of peers.

In some of the following contexts the teacher or counselor can make good use of psychodramatic methods:

1. *Discussion of class material,* that is, historical, literary, or contemporary social problems. Classes on the more complex personal relations involved in family life education programs may use role-playing materials to explore dating and marriage relationships, conflict resolution, and so on.

2. *Creative dramatics* is a field that is receiving widespread attention in many contemporary school settings, especially in Great Britain. However, the effectiveness of creative dramatics is in direct proportion to the degree to which the children are allowed to throw away their scripts and begin to improvise.

3. *Special situations.* Community crises relating to interracial strife, drug abuse programs, parent–student conflicts, or other issues of current attention can often become the focus of a sociodrama in a classroom or at an entire school assembly.

4. *Special education.* In special classes for children with learning disabilities, psychodramatic methods are used to help with the common problems of defeatism, behavior problems, and poor self-esteem. These special education classes include children who have specific learning disabilities, are severely emotionally disturbed or psychotic, or have behavior problems of hyperactivity.

   A common theme of concern to children in special education is that of being "different." This problem can be dealt with using role-playing as part of group discussions. Other children who can benefit from exploring the emotional aspects of their disease are those with asthma, diabetes, deafness, blindness, or other crippling handicaps.

5. *Affective education.* One of the most important developments in contempoary education is the attention being given to affective education, that is, the development of coping skills in interpersonal relationships and understanding feelings in oneself. The use of psychodramatic methods can catalyze this education for human awareness.

The use of psychodramatic methods in the schools has many potential benefits, if the approach is modified appropriately to the task at hand.

IV. PROFESSIONAL TRAINING

An important area for the applications of psychodramatic methods is in the development of interpersonal skills and sensitivity for students in training for the helping professions. Teachers, nurses, pastors, policemen, medical students, and many other groups can best deal with some items in their training through experiential rather than didactic modes of education (Figure 24).

For example, the problem of death and bereavement in our culture was one of the items brought up in a postgraduate development program for a group of nursery school teachers. Using psychodrama, the experience of grieving was explored. One teacher in the group started by asking how to deal with a child's questions about death. This led to another one of the teacher's enacting the loss of a spouse, which

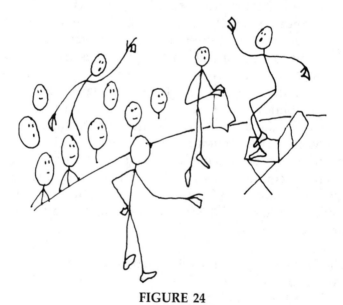

FIGURE 24

catalyzed a dramatic and emotion-filled catharsis by many of the teachers as they shared their own experiences of mourning. The results were: (1) a heightening of each group member's ability to help others with bereavement by using the empathy that arises from contact with personal feelings; (2) an awareness of the importance of sharing the experience, talking about the feelings of grief rather than avoiding the issue, of the need for touching and physical contact; and (3) an increased tolerance and openness not only to the experience of grief in the group members themselves and others, but also tolerance for the defenses against the expression of grief. These experiences enabled the group members to relate to the children and each other with greater authenticity.

Certainly, the problem of learning to help others grieve demands an experiential form of training. Nurses, medical personnel, and others who must deal with this reality in their work could benefit from understanding the stressful situation through roleplaying.

Not only is the problem of bereavement an issue for experiential training, but the problem of learning to help others with any complex role transition is a challenge in education. The plight of the young mother, the father of his first newborn, the man who has suffered a small stroke, the prospect of compulsory retirement are all subjects that involve a wide range of status changes and the demand for shifts in role behavior and values. Those who are in training for positions in which they will be helping people with life crises such as these would benefit from participating in role-playing situations that are part of discussion seminars.

V. APPLICATIONS IN INDUSTRY

Psychodrama itself would rarely be appropriate for most work situations, for the same reason that one should not use psychodrama in the classroom: a context with co-workers usually has more internal competition and distrust than people may wish to admit to themselves. Limited applications of psychodramatic methods, however, such as the use of roleplaying and action techniques, are widely used in industrial psychological consulting.

As in the fields of professional training, the major application of role playing in industry is to develop the skills of managers and the personnel and salesstaff. In addition, sociodramatic skills are often useful in resolving some of the more informal management–labor conflicts or other difficulties in communication. Most important, however, is the challenge of developing a broader imagination as to the implications of industry's actions in contemporary society and the building of psychological–interpersonal sophistication in management.

The potential director of role playing in an organization must become aware of the fundamental principles of consultation, the different needs of the clients, and the many competing agendas of the group (see Chapter 7). Nevertheless, if the management consultant is well-trained, knowledge of appropriate psychodramatic methods can vastly extend the effectiveness of the work.

VI. APPLICATIONS IN RELIGION

It is interesting to note that Moreno's ideas about creativity and spontaneity were first reflected in his poetic and theological works, which were written before he ever developed the psychodramatic method as a psychotherapeutic technique. Moreno's writings about the dynamic encounter between a human being and God in a co-creative relationship take on new relevance today, as contemporary religious trends expand to include ideas from other philosophies.

Moreno's word for enactments that deal with ultimate values and concerns is *axiodrama*. Through modifications of psychodramatic methods, a minister can search for more vivid and personal ways to help others to experience the challenge and significance of prayer, meditation, death, ethics, and so forth.

Some possible enactments that could be used as an introduction to a religious psychodrama include: (1) the relationship between Jesus and Judas; (2) the Grand Inquisitor (Dostoyevsky's story within *The Brothers Karamazov*); (3) the judgment in Heaven (Chapter 5); or (4) creation of a ritual for Christmas or Passover that is personally meaningful.

SUMMARY

Psychodramatic methods can be applied to achieve many kinds of goals and in a variety of contexts. This chapter has presented some of the major categories in which psychodramatic methods can be used, as well as providing references related to each area of application. Table 1 will be helpful in reviewing several key issues.

TABLE 1 Dimensions of Personal Development that May be Enhanced Through the Use of Psychodramatic Methods

Self-awareness

Clarification of inner feelings, goals, strengths, weaknesses, needs, fears
Growth of a wider role repertoire, more realistic body image, awareness of
  one's own interpersonal style, habitual responses
Sense of responsibility and ego boundaries strengthened

Interpersonal skills

Greater capacity for trust, autonomy, initiative, self-disclosure, self-
  assertion

(continued)

TABLE 1 (*continued*)

Increased awareness of other people's weaknesses, fears, needs, temper-
    amental differences
Knowledge of some common interactional and semantic communication
    difficulties; ability to express oneself congruently and clearly
The ability to listen, empathize, with less distortion

Value systems

Philosophy of life, some idea about the meaning of one's own death,
    significance of life, relations with spiritual concerns, engagement in
    nonrational experiences, meditation

Spontaneity

Playfulness, improvisation, participation in art, song, dance, drama,
    humor, wonder

Sensory–awakening

Body movement, sense of rhythm, points of balance, appropriate use of
    touch and sensuality

Imagination

Cultivation of skills in using associations, dreams, symbols, images,
    guided fantasy, intuition, storytelling in personal growth

REFERENCES

A. Inpatient Treatment

Anzieu, D. (1982). Psychodrama as technique of the psychoanalysis of
    institutions. In M. Pines and L. Rafaelsen (Eds.), *The individual and
    the group: Boundaries and interrelations* (Vol 1: Theory) (pp. 379–387).
    New York: Plenum Press.
Buchanan, D. R., and Dubbs-Siroka, J. (1980). Psychodramatic treatment
    for psychiatric patients. *National Association of Private Psychiatric Hos-
    pitals Journal*, 11(2), 27–31.
DiCori, F. (1977). Psychodrama in a hospital setting. In S. Arieti and G.
    Chrzanowski (Eds.), *New dimensions in psychiatry: A world view* (Vol.
    2, pp. 273–304). New York: John Wiley & Sons.

Gonen, J. (1971). The use of psychodrama combined with videotape play-back on an inpatient floor. *Psychiatry, 34*(2), 198–213.

Johnson, D. R. (1984). Representation of the internal world in catatonic schizophrenia. *Psychiatry, 47,* 299–314.

Jones, M. (1953). *The therapeutic community* (pp. 63–66). New York: Basic Books (Psychodrama was used as part of this pioneering experiment.)

Ossorio, A., and Fine, L. (1960). Psychodrama as a catalyst for social change in a mental hospital. In J. Masserman and J. L. Moreno (Eds.), *Progress in Psychotherapy* (Vol. 5). New York: Grune & Stratton.

Ploeger, A. (1982). The therapeutic community and the psychodrama, relations and countereffect in the therapeutic process. In M. Pines and L. Rafaelsen (Eds.), *The individual and the group* (pp. 193–197). New York: Plenum Press.

Polansky, N. A., and Harkins, E. B. (1969). Psychodrama as an element in hospital treatment. *Psychiatry, 32*(1), 74–87.

Rabiner, C. J., and Drucker, M. (1967). Use of psychodrama with hospital-ized schizophrenic patients. *Diseases of the Nervous System, 28,* 34.

Sakles, C. (1968). The place of psychodrama in an inpatient psychiatric treatment program. *Group Psychotherapy, 21*(4), 235–240.

Schatzberg, A., Lobis, R., and Westfall, M. P. (1974). The use of psychodrama in the hospital setting. *American Journal of Psychotherapy, 28*(4), 553–565.

Solomon, M. L., and Solomon, C. K. (1970). Psychodrama as an ancillary therapy on a psychiatric ward. *Canadian Psychiatric Association Journal, 15,* 365–373.

Williams, R. L., and Gasdick, J. M. (1970). Practical applications of psychodrama with chronic patients. *International Handbook of Sociometry, 21*(2), 192–193.

B. Alcoholism and Chemical Dependency

Blume, S. (1977). Psychodrama in the treatment of alcoholism. In N. Estes and E. Heinemann (Eds.), *Alcoholism, development, consequences and interventions.* St. Louis: C. V. Mosby.

Blume, S. (1978). Psychodrama and the treatment of alcoholism. In S. Zimberg, J. Wallace and S. Blume (Eds.), *Practical approaches to alcohol-ism psychotherapy* (pp. 77–97). New York: Plenum.

Blume, S. B., Robins, J. and Branston, A. (1968). Psychodrama techniques in the treatment of alcoholism. *Group Psychotherapy, 21*(4), 241–246.

Catanzaro, R. J. (1967). Tape-a-drama in treating alcoholics. *Quarterly Journal of Studies in Alcoholism, 28*(1), 138–140.

Olsson, P. A. (1972). Psychodrama and group therapy with young heroin addicts returning from duty in Vietnam. *Group Psychotherapy & Psychodrama, 25*(4), 141–147.

Van Gee, S. J. (1979, August). Alcoholism and the family: A psychodramatic approach. *Journal of Psychiatric Nursing, 8,* 9–12.

VanMeulenbrouck, M. (1973). Serial psychodrama with alcoholics. *Group Psychotherapy, 25*(4), 151–154.

Weiner, H. (1965). Treating the alcoholic with psychodrama. *Group Psychotherapy, 18*(1–2), 27–29.

Weiner, H. (1967). Psychodramatic treatment for the alcoholic. In R. Fox (Ed.), *Alcoholism: Behavioral research, therapeutic approaches.* New York: Springer Publishing Co.

Wood, D., Del Nouvo, A., Bucky, S. F., Schein, S., and Michalik, M. (1979). Psychodrama with an alcohol abuser population. *Group Psychotherapy, Psychodrama, & Sociometry, 32,* 75–88.

C. Outpatient Group Psychotherapy

Aveline, M. (1979, July). Action techniques in psychotherapy. *British Journal of Hospital Medicine,* 78–84.

Beagan, D. (1985). Spontaneity and creativity in the NHS: Starting a new group—psychodrama with adult day patients. *British Journal of Occupational Therapy, 48*(12), 370–374.

Blatner, H. (1968). Goal-orientation and action-orientation as two criteria for patient selection in group psychotherapy. *Voices, 4*(3), 90–95.

Collison, C. R., and Miller, S. L. (1985). The role of family re-enactment in group psychotherapy. *Perspectives in Psychiatric Care, 23*(2), 74–78.

Masters, G. (1978). Psychodrama: Learning to communicate. *Nursing Times, 74*(9), 350–352.

Mintz, E. E. (1974). On the dramatization of psychoanalytic interpretations. In Lewis R. Wolberg & M. L. Aronson (Eds.), *Group therapy, 1974.* New York: Stratton Intercontinental Medical Book Corp.

Naar, R. (1982). *A primer of group psychotherapy* (pp. 177–203). New York: Human Sciences Press.

Nicholas, M. W. (1984). *Change in the context of group therapy.* New York: Brunner/Mazel. (This book includes some good theory about how psychodrama may be integrated with other modern therapies and psychologies.)

Shaffer, J. B., and Galinsky, M. D. (1974). *Models of group therapy and sensitivity training* (pp. 108–127). Englewood Cliffs, NJ: Prentice-Hall.

D. Family Therapy

Compernolle, T. (1981). J. L. Moreno: An unrecognized pioneer of family therapy. *Family Process, 20,* 331–335.

Drake, B. (1975). Psychoanalytically oriented psychodrama with multiple family groups. *American Journal of Orthopsychiatry, 45*(2), 260–261.

Guldner, C. A. (1982). Multiple family psychodramatic therapy. *Journal of Group Psychotherapy, Psychodrama, & Sociometry, 35*(2), 47–56.

Hollander, C. E. (1983). Comparative family systems of Moreno and Bowen. *Journal of Group Psychotherapy, Psychodrama & Sociometry, 36*(1), 1–12.

Hollander, S. (1981). Spontaneity, sociometry, and the warming up process in family therapy. *Journal of Group Psychotherapy, Psychodrama, & Sociometry, 34,* 44–53.

Lee, R. H. (Summer, 1986). The family therapy trainer as coaching double. *Journal of Group Psychotherapy, Psychodrama & Sociometry, 39*(2), 52–57.

Perrott, L. (1986). Using psychodramatic techniques in structural family therapy. *Contemporary Family Therapy, 8*(4), 279–290.

Remer, R. (Spring, 1986). Use of psychodramatic intervention with families: Change on multiple levels. *Journal of Group Psychotherapy, Psychodrama, & Sociometry, 39*(1), 13–30.

Rozema, H. J., and Gray, M. A. (Spring, 1987). Stimulus activities for family communication. *Journal of Group Psychotherapy, Psychodrama, & Sociometry, 40*(1), 37–42.

Seeman, H., and Wiener, D. J. (1985). Comparing and using psychodrama with family therapy: Some cautions. *Journal of Group Psychotherapy, Psychodrama, & Sociometry, 37*(4), 143–157.

Starr, A. (1973). Sociometry of the family. In H. Mosak (Ed.), *Alfred Adler: His influence on psychology today.* Park Ridge, NJ: Noyes.

McKelvie, W. H. (1987). Kinetic family sculpture: Experiencing family change through time. *Individual Psychology: Journal of Adlerian Theory, Research & Practice, 43*(2), 160–173.

E. Child Psychotherapy and "In The Home"

Baum, N. (1973). Psychodrama and multi-media therapy with emotionally disturbed children. *Group Psychotherapy & Psychodrama, 26*(1–2), 48–66.

Barsky, M., and Mozenter, G. (1976). The use of creative drama in a children's group. *International Journal of Group Psychotherapy, 26,* 105–114.

Carpenter, P., and Sandberg, S. (1973). "The things inside": Psychodrama with delinquent adolescents. *Psychotherapy: Theory, Research and Practice, 10*(3), 245–247.

Creekmore, N. N., and Madan, A. J. (1981). The use of sociodrama as a therapeutic technique with behavior disordered children. *Behavioral Disorders, 7*(1), 28–33.

Geiser, R. L. (1971). An experimental program of activity therapy in a child care center. *Child Welfare, 50*(5), 290–297.

Goodrich, J., and Goodrich, W. (1986). Drama therapy with a learning disabled, personality disordered adolescent. *The Arts in Psychotherapy, 13,* 285–291.

Irwin, E. C. (1977). Play, fantasy, and symbols: Drama with emotionally disturbed children. *American Journal of Psychotherapy, 31*(3), 426–436.

Lockwood, J., and Harr, J. (1973). Psychodrama: A therapeutic tool with children in group play therapy. *Group Psychotherapy & Psychodrama, 26*(3–4), 53–67.

Mueller, E. E. (1971). Psychodrama with delinquent siblings. *Social Work, 11,* 18–28.

Robbins, M. (1973). Psychodramatic children's warm-ups for adults. *Group Psychotherapy & Psychodrama, 26*(1–2), 67–71.

Shearon, E. M. (1978). Psychodrama with children. *Group Psychotherapy, Psychodrama, & Sociometry, 33,* 142–155.

F. Adolescents and Delinquency

Altman, K. P. (1985). The role-taking interview: An assessment technique for adolescents. *Adolescence, 20*(80), 845–851.

Carpenter, P., and Sandberg, S. (1985). Further psychodrama with delinquent adolescents. *Adolescence, 20*(79), 599–604.

Godenne, G. D. (1965). Outpatient adolescent group psychotherapy: Use of co-therapists, psychodrama, and parent group therapy. *American Journal of Psychotherapy, 19*(1), 40–53.

Holmes, P. (1984). Boundaries or chaos: An outpatient psychodrama group for adolescents. *Journal of Adolescence, 7*(4), 387–400.

Jones, H. V. R. (1978). Psychodrama with adolescents. *Nursing Times, 74*(50), 2052–2054.

Leveton, E. (1984). *Adolescent Crisis* (pp. 77–79). New York: Springer Publishing Co.

Lockwood, J., and Harr, B. (1973). Psychodrama: A therapeutic tool with children in group play therapy. *Group Psychotherapy & Psychodrama, 26,* 53–67.

Olsson, P. A., and Myers, I. L. (1972). Nonverbal techniques in an adolescent group. *International Journal of Group Psychotherapy, 22*(2), 186–191.

Schramski, T. G., and Harvey, D. R. (1983). The impact of psychodrama and role playing in the correctional environment. *International Journal of Offender Therapy & Comparative Criminology, 27*(3), 243–254.

G. Mental Retardation

Buchan, L. G. (1972). *Roleplaying and the educable mentally retarded.* Belmont, CA: Fearon.

Klepac, R. L. (1978). Through the looking glass: Sociodrama and mentally retarded individuals. *Mental Retardation, 16*(5), 343–345.

Newburger, H. (1967). Psychodrama treatment with the brain damaged. *Group Psychotherapy, 20*(3), 129–130.

Pankratz, L., and Buchan, G. (1966). Techniques of warm-ups in psychodrama with the retarded. *Mental Retardation, 4*(5), 12–16.

Taylor, J. F. (1969). Role-playing with borderline and mildly retarded children in an institutional setting. *Exceptional Children, 36,* 206–208.

H. Miscellaneous Disabilities

Aach, S. (1976). Drama: A means of self-expression for the visually impaired child. *New Outlook for the Blind 70*(7), 282–285.

Altman, K. P. (1981). Psychodrama with blind psychiatric patients. *Journal of Visual Impairment & Blindness, 75*(4), 153–156.

Clayton, L., and Robinson, L. D. (1971). Psychodrama with deaf people. *American Annals of the Deaf, 116*(4), 415–419.

Swink, D. F. (1983). The use of psychodrama with deaf people. *Journal of Group Psychotherapy, Psychodrama & Sociometry, 36*(1), 23–29.

Schlanger, P. H., and Birkmann, M. H. (1978). Role playing used to elicit language from hearing impaired children. *Group Psychotherapy, Psychodrama, & Sociometry, 31,* 136–143.

Wolpe, Z. (1957). Play therapy, psychodrama, and parent counseling. In L. E. Travis (Ed.), *Handbook of speech pathology.* New York: Appleton-Century-Crofts.

I. Education

Amies, B., Warren, B., and Watling, R. (1986). *Social drama: Towards a therapeutic curriculum.* London: John Clare Books.

Chesler, M., and Fox, R. (1966). *Role-playing methods in the classroom.* Chicago: Science Research Associates.

Courtney, R. (1980). *The dramatic curriculum.* New York: Drama Book Specialists.

Garvey, D. M. (1967). Simulation, role-playing, and sociodrama in the social studies (with annotated bibliography). *Emporia State Research Studies, 16*(2), 5–34.

Lyons, V. (1977). Psychodrama as a counseling technique with children. *Elementary School Guidance and Counseling, 11*(4), 252–257.

Mathis, J. A., Fairchild, L., and Cannon, T. M. (1980). Psychodrama and sociodrama in primary and secondary education. *Psychology in the Schools, 17*(1), 96–101.

Nieminen, S. (1986). Using psychodramatic techniques as a means of preventive mental health work in Finland. *School Psychology International, 7*(2), 94–97.

Milroy, E. (1982). *Role-play: A practical guide.* Aberdeen, Scotland: Aberdeen University Press.

Shaftel, F., and Shaftel, G. (1982). *Role-playing in the curriculum* (2nd Ed.). Englewood Cliffs, NJ: Prentice-Hall. (This is a revised edition of their 1967 book, *Role playing for social values.*).

Shearon, E. M., and Shearon, W. (1973). Some uses of psychodrama in education. *Group Psychotherapy & Psychodrama, 26*(3–4), 47–53.

Stanford, G., and Roark, A. (1975). Role playing and action methods in the classroom. *Group Psychotherapy & Psychodrama, 28*, 33–49.

Van Mentz, M. (1983). *The effective use of role-play: A handbook for teachers and trainers.* London: Kogan Page.

Wells, C. G. (1962). Psychodrama and creative counseling in the elementary school. *Group Psychotherapy, 15*(3–4), 244–252.

J. Professional Training

Beglen, G. G. (1983). The use of psychodramatic and sociometric techniques in the in-service training of residential treatment child care staff. *Journal of Group Psychotherapy, Psychodrama, & Sociometry, 36*(1), 13–22.

Byrd, G. J., and Olsson, P. A. (March, 1975). The use of pedagogic drama in psychiatric education. *Journal of Medical Education, 50*, 299–300.

Darragh, E., and Gentles, R. (July, 1980). Role playing in leadership training. *Dimensions in Health Service,* 21–22.

Kipper, D. A., and Ben-Ely, Z. (1979). The effectiveness of the psychodramatic double method, the reflection method, and lecturing in the training of empathy. *Journal of Clinical Psychology, 35*(2), 370–375.

Kranz, P., and Huston, K. (1984). The use of psychodrama to facilitate supervisee development in Master's level counseling students. *Journal of Group Psychotherapy, Psychodrama, & Sociometry, 37*(3), 126–134.

Reed, E. J. (1984). Using psychodrama with critical care nurses. *Dimensions of Critical Care Nursing, 3*(2), 110–114

Thacker, A. K. (1984). Using psychodrama to reduce "burnout" or role fatigue in the helping professions. *Journal of Group Psychotherapy, Psychodrama, & Sociometry, 37*(1), 14–26.

Tomlinson, A., MacLeod-Clark, J., and Faulkner, A. (1984). Role Play. *Nursing Times, 80*(38–39), 45–51.

VanderMay, J., and Peake, T. (1980). Psychodrama as a psychotherapy supervision technique. *Group Psychotherapy, Psychodrama & Sociometry, 33*, 25–32.

K. Industry, Business, and Organizational Development

Argyris, C. (1951). *Role-playing in action.* (Bulletin No. 16). Ithaca, NY: Cornell University/New York State School of Industrial & Labor Relations.

Lippitt, R., and Hubbell, A. (1956). Role playing for personnel and guidance workers: Review of the literature. *Group Psychotherapy, 9*(2), 89–114.

Shaw, M. E., Corsini, R., Blake, R., & Mouton, J. (1980). *Role playing: A practical manual for group facilitators.* San Diego, CA: University Associates. (Excellent bibliography, oriented mainly to business and organizational audiences. This is a re-working of the 1961 edition titled *Role-playing in business and industry,* with Corsini as the first author.)

Stahl, G. (1958). Role-playing in industry. *Group Psychotherapy, 6*(3–4), 202–215.

Torrance, E. P., and Wright, J. A. (1987). Sociometric audience technique as a device for maximizing creativity in problem solving in large groups. *The Creative Child and Adult Quarterly, 12*(3), 147–151.

Wohlking, W., and Weiner, H. (1971). Structured and spontaneous role playing: Contrast and comparison. In W. Wohlking (Ed.), *Role playing: Its application in management development.* (pp. 1–11). New York: Cornell University.

L. Religion

Clayton, G. M. (1971). Sociodrama in a church group. *Group Psychotherapy & Psychodrama, 24*(3–4), 97–100.

DeCarvalho, E. S. (1986). Christian reconciliation: A psychodramatic contribution. *Journal of Psychology & Christianity, 5*(1), 5–10.

Hittson, H. (1970). Psychodrama in a church counseling program. *Group Psychotherapy & Psychodrama, 23*(1–2), 113–117.

Johnson, P. E. (1959). Interpersonal psychology of religion: Moreno and Buber. *Group Psychotherapy, 12,* 211–217.

Kraus, C. (1984). Psychodrama for fallen gods: A review of Morenean theology. *Journal of Group Psychotherapy, Psychodrama & Sociometry, 37*(2), 47–64.

Moreno, J. L. (1948). Experimental theology. *Sociatry, 2*(1–2), 93–98.

Nolte, J., Smallwood, C. and Weistart, J. (1975). Role reversal with God. *Group Psychotherapy & Psychodrama, 28,* 70–76.

Zacher, A. N. (1961). The use of psychodrama in pastoral therapy. *Group Psychotherapy, 14*(1–2), 164–168.

M. Criminal Justice System

Barocas, H. (1972). Psychodrama techniques in training police in family crisis intervention training. *Group Psychotherapy and Psychodrama, 25,* 30–31.

Buchanan, D. R. (March, 1981). Action methods for the criminal justice system. *Federal Probation,* 17–25.

Melnick, M. (1984). Skills through drama: The use of professional theater techniques in the treatment and education of prison and ex-offender populations. *Journal of Group Psychotherapy, Psychodrama, & Sociometry, 37*(3), 104–116.

Swink, D. F., Siegel, J., and Spodak, B. (1984). Saint Elizabeths Hospital Action Training Lab for Police. *Journal of Group Psychotherapy, Psychodrama, & Sociometry, 37*(3), 94–103.

N. With the Elderly

Altman, K. P. (1983). Psychodrama with the institutionalized elderly: A method for role re-engagement. *Journal of Group Psychotherapy, Psychodrama, & Sociometry, 36*(3), 87–96.

Buchanan, D. R. (1982). Psychodrama: A humanistic approach to psychiatric treatment for the elderly. *Hospital & Community Psychiatry, 33*(3), 220–223.

Burwell, D. (1977). Psychodrama and the depressed elderly. *The Canadian Nurse, 73*(4), 54–55.

Carman, M., and Nordin, S. (1984). Psychodrama: A therapeutic modality for the elderly in nursing homes. *Clinical Gerontologist, 3*(Fall), 15–24.

Johnson, D. R. (1986). The developmental method in drama therapy: Group treatment with the elderly. *Arts in Psychotherapy, 13*(1), 17–33.

Mazor, R. (1982). Drama therapy for the elderly in a day care center. *Hospital & Community Psychiatry, 33,* 577–579.

Nordin, S. R. (1987). Psychodrama with the elderly. *Journal of Group Psychotherapy, Psychodrama, & Sociometry, 40*(2), 51–61.

Sandel, S. L., and Johnson D. R. (1987). *Waiting at the gate: Creativity and hope in the nursing home.* New York: Haworth.

Telander, M., Quinlan, F., and Verson, K. (1987). *Acting up! An innovative approach to creative drama for older adults.* Morton Grove, IL: The Coach House Press.

Weisberg, N., and Wilder, R. (Eds.). (1986). *Drama with older adults: Therapeutic interventions.* New Haven: National Association of Drama Therapists.

9

Theoretical Issues in the Use of Psychodramatic Methods

Psychodrama is grounded in a number of theoretical concepts. A fundamental premise is that diagnosis and treatment must involve a broad range of dimensions of human experience, including such variables as nonverbal communications, systems-oriented dynamics of the interpersonal field, the richness of imagery, the power of insight, learning through action, and so forth. This represents an eclectic approach, but in this sense eclecticism is not a superficial grab bag of techniques. Contemporary efforts toward a rigorous intellectual integration of theory in psychotherapy reveal that eclecticism can offer a more holistic orientation that surpasses the narrow sectarianism of the competing "schools" of psychology.

Psychodramatic methods are to be viewed most realistically as functioning *within* an eclectic approach to the helping relationship. There are moments in any therapy for analysis, individual study, reflection, and careful planning, but at other times, human development demands a level of personal creativity that can best be achieved within a context of spontaneity, active participation, group support, and the freedom to explore many different facets of a situation.

Indeed, progress in psychology has increased our awareness of the number of factors involved in any human situation. These include variations in cognitive style, temperament, coping skills, cultural norms, and stages of life. Role dynamics is a theoretical framework I have created to address these multiple variables and to help facilitate the clinical application of role theory. It allows for an integration of many different schools of psychotherapy, now thought of as different ways of viewing the complexity of the human biopsychosocial and spiritual system. Role dynamics and other theoretical concepts are more fully developed in my book *Foundations of Psychodrama* (1988).

It is the purpose of this chapter to note *how* psychodramatic methods can facilitate the development of human potentialities in psychotherapy and education. Three major avenues of reasoning will be used: (1) that psychodramatic methods can be helpful in the process of emotional problem solving; (2) that the sense of self can be strengthened effectively by building a wider role repertoire using psychodramatic methods; and (3) that psychodramatic methods are consistent with and capable of being easily integrated with other psychotherapeutic methods.

EMOTIONAL PROBLEM SOLVING

Many of the decisions that we face daily require some consideration of the nonrational factors in our lives. Skills of introspection are needed in order to properly weigh and include the emotional dimensions of any situation. In order to gain a perspective on the unconscious determinants of one's choices, it is necessary to find ways of developing insight into interpersonal relationships. The use of psychodramatic methods can complement verbal methods in facilitating *the analysis of* the many different dimensions of emotional problem solving (Lebovici, 1957). The process of psychotherapy or education about feelings thus can be viewed in terms of: (1) establishing a context that maximizes the conditions of personal growth and (2) partially analyzing the modes of problem solving.

THE CONTEXT OF GROWTH

One of the most fundamental principles of any form of psychotherapy is the establishment of a healthy helping relationship. So much of what transpires in this context is based on the factor of *suggestion,* which, in turn, is affected by role behavior of the helper, the expectation of help, and by the client's acceptance of his own role as the one who is to be helped (Shearon, 1978). The presence of others who share the client's belief in the healing system (e.g., in a group setting) heightens the effectiveness of the suggestion factors of psychotherapy. The director who uses psychodramatic methods increases these suggestion factors by her active self-disclosure and skillful use of the dramatic dimensions of her approach.

A second psychotherapeutic factor begins to operate when the director establishes norms for the group: acceptance, permissiveness, honesty, self-observation, expectations of risk-taking, expressions of emotion, self-disclosure, discussion, mutuality, and so forth (Yalom, 1985). In psychodrama the director *models* these behaviors, as well as talks *about* them. The group process then functions on a fail-safe basis; the level of judgment by peers is reduced, and support for creativity and spontaneity is reinforced.

A further factor of therapy is the use of a specified time in a setting of sufficient length for each person to get involved. The use of psychodramatic methods demands more time than other approaches, because it recognizes the role of the warm-up. Time for warming up to the point of creativity and spontaneity is necessary in order to reach a level of emotional expression (catharsis) that will produce insight (Mintz, 1971).

The last point in establishing a context for growth is the use of the individual-centered format. Dealing with the problems of one protagonist at a time within a group setting has several advantages over the group-centered approach, in which the director deals primarily with issues of total group process (Perls, 1967). In the individual-centered approach, the protagonist presents a concrete example of a problem that is often representative of the group theme at the time; enactment helps to go beyond abstract discussion into the deeper feelings relating to a problem. The director then uses the group to facilitate the protagonist's emotional problem solving in several ways: as a source of confrontation, support, consensual feedback, concern, and reinforcement of the protagonist's adaptive behaviors (Sakles, 1973). Certainly the attention of the group increases the factors of positive concern and expectation (i.e., suggestion) for the protagonist's growth processes.

CLARIFICATION OF THE PROBLEM

Whether or not a group is used, the process of exploring and integrating the emotional dimensions of any problem is facilitated in many ways by using psychodramatic methods:

1. When the problem is presented, an enactment can help to bring out the *concrete behavior* that is involved. So many protagonists tend to habitually explain, intellectualize, or be defensively vague or circumstantial; concrete presentation circumvents these defenses. "Diagnosis" (i.e., seeing-through) is most effective when the director discovers some

of the dimensions of the situation that the protagonist might ignore or avoid in a verbal narrative. Recreating the event in an enactment can help the protagonist to stop explaining and just show what happened.

2. Once the situation is presented concretely in an enactment it usually becomes obvious to the observer that the protagonist is engaging in and/or reacting to nonverbal communications, many of which he is only dimly aware of. Using psychodramatic methods, the director helps the protagonist to become explicitly aware of these gestures, expressions, and postures. Incongruities between verbal and nonverbal communications often account for a major portion of the difficulties encountered in interpersonal relationships. For example, a mother's statement to her children, "Go ahead and have a good time—don't worry about me," if accompanied by a pained expression, usually evokes a response of feeling guilty and worrying about mother. Furthermore, the exploration of the meanings of the protagonist's own nonverbal communication can become an avenue for self-confrontation of character defenses—an essential step toward insight (see Chapter 5). There are many other action methods that can be utilized to help the protagonist to view his own behavior more objectively, as well as to think about the impact that the behavior has on others.

3. Psychodramatic methods rapidly move the protagonist into the emotional levels of his problem. Through dramatization, the use of supportive doubling, and the judicious use of physical contact in an enactment, the protagonist *experiences* the feelings as well as talks about them. Of course, the use of touching, whether it be in holding, patting, or shoving, must be carefully applied, for it is a very powerful avenue to the evocation of emotion (Forer, 1969; Mintz, 1969). Yet, if the director is skillful and works in a mutual relationship with the protagonist, she can greatly extend the effectiveness of the participatory learning experience.

The many methods noted in Chapters 4, 5, and 6 can help the protagonist not only to discuss but also to actively *experience* the issues at hand, which is the whole point of participatory and experiential education.

4. The process of emotional problem solving requires consideration not only of the protagonist's feelings, but also of the feelings of the others with whom he is interacting. The development of an *empathic understanding* can be facilitated by actually having the protagonist enact the role of the other person. Through role reversal, the protagonist discovers many viewpoints that expand his own insight and help him to choose more adaptive responses.

5. Finally, the discussion as to possible solutions in problem-solving can be extended into active working through; not only are the new ideas talked about, but by using psychodramatic methods, they *are tried out in a simulated situation*. The group members can then *model* the behaviors they suggest. Successful and spontaneous behaviors are reinforced, while ineffective adaptations become immediately apparent and are gradually extinguished (Sturm, 1970). The group's tolerant support provides a corrective emotional experience. All of these components of working through are made more vivid through adding psychodramatic to the verbal–analytic methods.

FUNCTION OF SURPLUS REALITY

If the use of psychodramatic methods in dealing with emotional problem solving seems "artificial" or "gimmicky," it may be due to a common misunderstanding as to the role of *surplus reality* in our lives. The view of human beings as *only* existentially being-in-the-world, with one unified core of authenticity, denies the phenomenon of imagination. It is our imagination that accounts for the self-reflective dimensions of our consciousness, the ability to see ourselves at a distance. Humans are the only animals who become embarrassed, who consider their own death, who do not learn from experience (because they cling to their illusions). These aspects of our essential humanity are manifestations of the imagination.

The imagination represents that dimension of our lives that is our *surplus reality*. We are kings, we are slaves; we are again children, we exist 10 years in the future. The invitation to utilize our imagination, to say, "if . . ." is the essence of play, hypnosis, and psychodrama (Blatner & Blatner, 1988).

I maintain that the willingness to suspend disbelief in order to permit a period of fantasy is not artificial. Nor, when explicitly chosen, is the involvement in imagination a regressive function. Indeed, the modality of play is a powerful and, at times, essential vehicle to (1) provide some distance and ego protection, (2) change attitudinal set, (3) function as an intermediary between the polarities of fully committed action and passive reflection; subjectivity and objectivity; the aesthetic and the pragmatic; spontaneity and calculation, etc.; and (4) especially, through use of imagery, play serves as an avenue for entrance into the complex world of feelings, mythologic complexes, and spiritual dimensions.

The use of psychodramatic techniques is thus becoming an important approach for the use of imagination as a function in personal development.

EXPANSION OF THE ROLE REPERTOIRE

A second major argument for the use of psychodramatic methods rests on the basis not of psychodynamic theory, but of *role* theory. The view of humans as evolving along many simultaneous dimensions is a basic premise (Moreno, 1961). Furthermore, psychopathology reflects not only a distortion of one of these aspects of personality, but often represents a compensatory expression of one facet of the personality primarily due to a lack of development of another. For example, a person with few opportunities, or validation for building skills in the realm of imagination and feelings, tends to become over intellectualized. The intellectualization is a "vacuum activity" (a term borrowed from ethology, referring to the time-filling behavior of animals when their normal outlets are frustrated, such as by being in a cage.)

Psychotherapy and education viewed from the position of role theory would emphasize the training of the person's capacity in a variety of roles that can balance and complement each other. The normal function of play in childhood is to at least symbolically enact a wide variety of roles that then become a core of identifications and ego strengths (Sarbin, 1943). For example, the child must play at being a mother before he or she can convert internalized nurturing behaviors given by the parents into an active sense of nurturing others.

A more comprehensive exploration of role theory will be presented in my book on role dynamics. Suffice it to say that I believe it is necessary for people to build a wide role repertoire, including a variety of forms of skills (see Table 1, p. 121).

The use of psychodramatic methods can be an effective form of engaging in learning about these many roles, rather than simply talking about them. Psychodramatic role playing is a major form of *experiential* and *participatory* education, and education is a major aspect of a total psychotherapeutic program.

Some specific ways in which developing a wider role repertoire may function are:

1. *The sense of choice* is increased, as there are more behavioral roles with which one is familiar.

2. *The importance of many different aspects of life* is validated through role-taking behaviors: dimensions such as play, dance, achievement, competition, imagination.
3. *Identification.* The practice in taking other roles builds an increased capacity for empathy. Meerloo (1966) writes, "Partaking in the psyche of the other means using the vicarious signs of preverbal communication. Moreno, the founder of modern group therapy, calls this mutual partaking and emotional communicative understanding from afar 'telic sensitivity' and 'telic-reciprocity.' "
4. *Experiencing the sense of self.* Taking active and creatively spontaneous role behaviors in many dimensions fulfills an extremely important function: that of validating the sense of one's own vitality, will, authenticity, feelings, imagery, and, in short, the sense of being deeply alive, of being a "self."
5. *Flexibility.* Role-taking behavior, if reinforced, helps people to allow themselves to develop a sense of mastery in many different role situations: father, lover, daughter, judge, student, friend, teacher, police officer. In turn, the components of each role can be applied more easily in new situations where synthesis must be developed.

INTEGRATION WITH OTHER PSYCHOTHERAPEUTIC APPROACHES

Within the general framework of eclecticism as noted at the beginning of this chapter, I consider the various theoretical systems of psychotherapy and their practical methodologies as being essentially compatible with each other. Each approach relates best to only a few facets of human experience, and a flexible application of several different methods may be required in the individualized treatment of each case. Moreover, the synthesis of two methods often can result in significantly greater effectiveness than could be obtained from either method being used alone.

For example, the psychodynamics of the Oedipal conflict as described by psychoanalytic theory may often emerge spontaneously within a psychodrama. This phenomenon has been capitalized upon by some orthodox psychoanalysts in France, who use several therapists in creating psychodrama for selected patients (Lebovici et al., 1952). The interactional dynamics as described by Sullivan, Adler, and Eric Berne can often be illustrated to a family or group by recreating the conflict situations in a psychodramatic enactment (Jacobs, 1977; Naar, 1977).

The theoretical concepts relating to ego-splitting (in object-relations theory), complexes (in Jungian theory) (Whitmont, 1984) and autonomous body language (in Gestalt therapy) all can be made more demonstrable by objectifying parts of the person's psyche in psychodramatic enactment (Orcutt, 1977). The conflicting facets of the personality are then helped to symbolically encounter each other in an effort to reach a constructive resynthesis of the personality.

Other therapeutic systems that have much in common with the psychodramatic method include George Kelly's *role perscriptions* in his *Theory of Personal Constructs* (Bonney & Scott, 1983); the system of *Direct Analysis* as practiced by John Rosen; and the ritualized activities of traditional practitioners of non-Western medicine in other cultures (Fryba, 1972; Harmeling, 1950).

In addition to therapies that are dramatic in their quality, there are also many approaches that utilize subtler aspects of role playing or other psychodramatic techniques. The techniques of assertion training in the behavior therapies, and of "sidetaking" in conjoint family therapy are both essentially psychodramatic in their process. In addition, psychodramatic methods are frequently being used as an integral part of many therapy groups that use transactional analysis, reality therapy (Greenberg & Bassin, 1976), psychosynthesis, or bioenergetics as their main orientation. Indeed, I am aware of professionals in almost every facet of education, organizational development, and psychotherapy who have been able to creatively adapt psychodramatic methods to the requirements of their tasks.

SUMMARY

The theoretical basis of the use of psychodramatic methods rests on a foundation of eclecticism in the choice of psychotherapeutic and educational approaches. Psychodramatic methods may be more specifically applied for two purposes: analysis and synthesis. As an analytic agent, psychodrama can be invaluable in clarifying the person's dynamics at every stage in the process of emotional problem solving. In the task of ego synthesis, psychodramatic methods may be applied to facilitate the development of a widened repertoire and as an aid in generating skills for using the imagination. Finally, by enabling the participants to engage in trial behaviors within a fail-safe context, symbolic ventilation and reinforcement of new learning can occur.

Many of the contemporary psychotherapies utilize a combination of analytic and synthesizing processes. Most of these approaches may become even more effective through the use of psychodramatic methods, either as an adjunct or as an integral component of their therapeutic practice.

REFERENCES

Allport, G. W. (1968). The fruits of eclecticism, bitter or sweet? In G. Allport, *The person in psychology: Selected essays*. Boston: Beacon.

Bischof, L. J., and Moreno, J. (1964). In L. J. Bischof (Ed.), *Interpreting personality theories* (pp. 355–420). New York: Harper & Row.

Blatner, A. (1985). The dynamics of catharsis. *Journal of Group Psychotherapy, Psychodrama, & Sociometry, 37*(4), 157–166.

Blatner, A. (1988). Foundations of psychodrama: History, theory, and practice. New York: Springer Publishing Co.

Blatner, A., and Blatner, A. (1988). *The art of play: An adult's guide to reclaiming imagination and spontaneity.* New York: Human Sciences Press.

Blatner, H. A. (1969–70). Theoretical aspects of psychodrama—general comments. *Bulletin de Psychologie, 23*(285), 13–16.

Bonney, W. C., and Scott, K. H. (1983). An exploration of the origin of role formation via psychodrama and personal construct theories. *Journal of Group Psychotherapy, Psychodrama, & Sociometry, 36*(2), 47–54.

Buchanan, D. R., and Little, D. (1983). Neuro-linguistic programming and psychodrama: Theroretical and clinical similarities. *Journal of Group Psychotherapy, Psychodrama, & Sociometry, 36*(3), 114–122.

Elm, A. C. (Ed.) (1969). *Role-playing, reward and attitude change.* New York: Van Nostrand Insight.

Forer, B. (1969). The taboo against touching in psychotherapy. *Psychotherapy: Theory, Research and Practice, 6*(5), 225–231.

Fryba, M. (1972). Psychodrama elements in psychosis treatment by shamans of Sri Lanka. In M. Pines & L. Rafaelsen (Eds.), *The individual and the group: Boundaries and interrelations* (Vol 2: Practice) (pp. 333–339). New York: Plenum Press.

Ginn, I.L.B. (1973). Catharsis: Its occurrence in Aristotle, psychodrama, and psychoanalysis. *Group Psychotherapy & Psychodrama, 26*(2), 7–22.

Gosnell, D. (1964). Some similarities and dissimilarities between the psychodramaturgical approaches of J. L. Moreno and Erving Goffman. *International Journal of Sociometry and Sociatry, 3,* 94–106.

Greenberg, I., and Bassin, A. (1976). Reality therapy and psychodrama. In A. Bassin, T. Bratter, and R. Rachin (Eds.), *The reality therapy reader* (pp. 231–240). New York: Harper & Row.

Gumina, J. M., Gonen, J. V., and Hagen, J. (1973). Implosive psychodrama. *Group Psychotherapy & Psychodrama, 26*(1–2), 97–106.

Harmeling, P. C. (1950). Therapeutic theatre of Alaska Eskimos. *Group Psychotherapy, 3*(1–2), 74–75.

Jacobs, A. (1977). Psychodrama and TA. In M. James (Ed.), *Techniques in transactional analysis for therapists and counselors* (pp. 239–249). Reading, MA: Addison-Wesley.

Jeammet, P., and Kestemberg, E. (1983). Le psychodrame psychanalytique a l'adolescence. *Adolescence, 1*(1), 147–163.

Kellerman, P. F. (1983). Resistance in psychodrama. *Journal of Group Psychotherapy, Psychodrama, & Sociometry, 36*(1), 30–43.

Kelly, G. R. (1978). Behaviorism and psychodrama: Worlds not so far apart. *Group Psychotherapy, Psychodrama, & Sociometry, 31,* 154–162.

Kelly, G. R. (1982). Theoretical applications of symbolic interactionism and psychodrama. *Journal of Group Psychotherapy, Psychodrama, & Sociometry, 35*(1), 39–45.

Kreitler, H., and Eblinger, S. (1968). Validation of psychodramatic behavior against behavior in life. *British Journal of Medical Psychology, 41,* 185.

Lebovici, S. (1957). Uses of psychodrama in psychiatric diagnosis. *International Journal of Sociometry and Sociatry, 1*(4), 175–180.

Lebovici, S., Diatkine, R., and Kestemberg, E. (1952). Applications of psychoanalysis to group psychotherapy and psychodrama therapy in France. *Group Psychotherapy, 5,* 39–50.

Meerloo, J.A.M. (1966). Why do we sympathize with each other? *Archives of General Psychiatry, 15,* 390–397.

Mintz, E. E. (1969). On the rationale of touch in psychotherapy. *Psychotherapy: Theory, Research and Practice, 6*(4), 232–235.

Mintz, E. E. (1971). *Marathon groups: Symbol and reality.* New York: Appleton-Century-Crofts.

Moreno, J. L. (1961). The role concept: A bridge between psychiatry and sociology. *American Journal of Psychiatry, 118,* 518–523.

Naar, R. (1977). A psychodramatic intervention with a T.A. framework in individual and group psychotherapy. *Group Psychotherapy, Psychodrama & Sociometry,, 30,* 127–134.

O'Connell, W. E. (1969). Teleodrama. *The Individual Psychologist, 6*(2), 42–45.

Orcutt, T. L. (1977). Roles and rules: The kinship and territoriality of psychodrama and gestalt therapy. *Group Psychotherapy, Psychodrama, & Sociometry, 30,* 97–107.

Ortman, H. (1966). How psychodrama fosters creativity. *Group Psychotherapy, 19* (3–4), 201–213.

Perls, F. S. (1967). Workshop vs individual therapy. *Journal of Long Island Consultation Center, 5*(2), 13–17.

Sakles, C. J. (1973). Role conflict and transference in combined psychodramatic group therapy and individual psychoanalytically-oriented psychotherapy. *Group Psychotherapy & Psychodrama, 26*(3–4), 70–76.

Sarbin, T. R. (1943). The concept of role-taking. *Sociometry, 6,* 243.

Seeman, H. (1982). A methodology for existential psychotherapy: Psychodrama. *Journal of Group Psychotherapy, Psychodrama, & Sociometry, 35*(2), 70–82.

Shearon, E. M. (1978). Aspects of persuasion in psychodrama. *Group Psychotherapy, Psychodrama, & Sociometry, 31*, 96–108.

Shearon, E. M. (1981). Comparison of Rogers' self theory and Moreno's spontaneity theory. *Journal of Group Psychotherapy, Psychodrama, & Sociometry, 34*, 112–133.

Sturm, I. E. (1970). A behavioral outline of psychodrama. *Psychotherapy: Theory, Research and Practice, 7*(4), 245–247.

Whitmont, E. C. (1984). Recent influences on the practice of Jungian analysis. In M. Stein (Ed.), *Jungian Analysis* (pp. 346–360). Boulder, CO: Shambhala.

Yalom, I. (1985). *Theory and practice of group psychotherapy* (3rd Ed.). New York: Basic Books.

10

The Training of the Psychodramatist

The practice of psychodrama is one of the most challenging forms in the field of clinical behavioral science. As a complex method of psychotherapy, and because of its power, practitioners must obtain extensive training. While some of the component methods such as role reversal may be integrated into the process of most forms of psychotherapy, the full use of psychodrama, involving warm-up, action, and closure, requires more than a mere knowledge of the techniques.

Part of the art of using the method is that it must be applied with the sensitivity of a trained psychotherapist; therefore, one of the requirements for certification as a practitioner by the American Board of Examiners in Psychodrama, Sociometry, and Group Psychotherapy is that each person complete the equivalent of a master's level program in a discipline that is generally acknowledged as a basis for practicing psychotherapy. A basic knowledge of the principles of psychopathology, psychotherapy, and related subjects is necessary for learning to use this method in clinical settings.

After Moreno's death in 1974, the control of the American Society of Group Psychotherapy and Psychodrama (ASGPP) shifted naturally to the democratically elected executive committee. Zerka Moreno released her residual power and allowed the committee to assume responsibility for the organization. She began to develop and teach psychodrama in her own way, thus carrying on the work with renewed creativity. The ASGPP decided to promote the overall level of professionalism in psychodrama by establishing a certifying board, similar to other specialties and disciplines. In 1976, the American Board of Examiners in Psychodrama, Sociometry, and Group Psychotherapy was established, and two levels of competence were designated: *Practitioner,* and *Trainer, Educator, and Practitioner (T.E.P).* The Board has developed criteria for certification and administers examinations for applicants. It continues to revise its program to meet the changing needs of this subspecialty and the larger evolving professional climate.

The importance of establishing credentials in this field is especially important because there are many people who use related techniques and claim they are doing psychodrama without proper training. They may have attended one or a few workshops and think they can do it too, not infrequently with negative results. The method is then blamed, rather than the incompetence of the group leader.

This is a common problem in any new field. It is tempting to think one knows what one is doing when in fact one does not know. Watching a trained professional directing a psychodrama can appear to be a deceptively simple task. Actually, it is the most complex form of psychotherapy. If you want to learn this method you should obtain training from an accredited teacher of psychodrama; in addition, if professionals offer to direct you in a psychodrama, carefully inquire about their credentials.

WHERE TO OBTAIN TRAINING

As of this writing, there are approximately 100 certified trainers of psychodrama in the United States. This is the highest credential in psychodrama and is designated with the title

"Trainer, Educator, and Practitioner," abbreviated as T.E.P. (There are an estimated equal number of trainers in other countries around the world.) In addition, there are another 200–300 professionals who are certified to direct psychodrama at the "Practitioner" level. (Internationally, the numbers are probably in the thousands.)

The Board of Examiners has become the appropriate source of up-to-date names and addresses of T.E.P.s, Practitioners and training institutes. These can be obtained by writing to The American Board of Examiners in Psychodrama, Group Psychotherapy, & Sociometry, P.O. Box 15552, Washington, DC 20052; inquiries may also be sent to: The American Society for Group Psychotherapy & Psychodrama (ASGPP), 6728 Old McLean Village Drive, McLean, VA 22101, Phone: (1-703) 556–9222.

THE ELEMENTS OF TRAINING

The development of the skill of psychodrama involves the learning of a good deal of factual material, combined with a great deal of experience in the roles of protagonist, auxiliary ego, co-director, and, with supervision, as director. The reading list of the American Board of Examiners is updated periodically and contains many of the most significant materials for students who want to prioritize their studies. Attendance at weekend workshops, ongoing courses, and practicum experiences are typical examples of experiential modes of learning. For those who aspire to certification, the majority of these teaching experiences should be from professionals accredited at the "Trainer" (T.E.P.) level by the Board.

Gradually, the student will begin to direct small enactments, situation tests, or circumscribed role-playing activities under supervision as soon as he or she is able. Also, psychodramatic methods may be introduced as facilitating agents in the course of more traditional ongoing group or family therapy. At first the use of these active approaches requires a degree of risk taking, but this is necessary in order to develop a sense of competence, as the assimilation and accommodation elements in learning require the full use of the body as well as the mind. Moreno noted that insight occurs through the muscles as well as the mind, a sentiment that resonates with the educational psychology of John Dewey.

In the course of training, there are a number of ways that the student of psychodrama can be aided by the teacher (Goldman et al., 1982; Nolte & Hale, 1976). Theories of psychodrama can be used to help the apprentice director to bring out the group's main concern and relate this to the work of the protagonist (Buchanan, 1980).

A related mode of learning involves the development of role-taking skills in general. Role taking can become an ongoing type of discipline: When encountering another person in the context of conversation, explore the nature of some of the other person's roles. The questions you ask are expressions of your actively imaging what it might be like to be in the role being discussed: What are its advantages and disadvantages? What events occur that evoke emotions such as enjoyment or sadness, anxiety or irritation (Blatner & Blatner, 1988)? The impact of this technique, used with discretion, is that of being empathic and involved. It is fun to talk with people who are willing to enter one's experiential world.

Similarly, with colleagues, explore the nature of unfamiliar frames of reference. As a therapist, consider the patient's point of view, and that of the patient's family members. Work from what Carl Rogers called "the self-system."

One group of concepts that is particularly useful is that of the "defense mechanisms." These are subconscious, magical, somewhat primitive forms of thinking, and they can be expressed not only in descriptive prose, but also in the form of dialog—i.e., the "self system" mentioned above. In fact, these cognitive transformations are often utilized on a pre-verbal or nonverbal level, but they have a cognitive equivalent. A sullen withdrawal may have no conscious equivalent, but it functions *as if* to say, "I'm not going to budge. You should reach out to me," or "Leave me alone, everything you do just makes me feel worse."

Learn the various defense mechanisms, these various forms of self-deceptions, manipulations, and characterologic elaborations that express the "hidden" levels of feeling and communication. Knowing them, bringing them out in the role of double, helps a psychodramatic enactment to portray the greater "truth" that in real life goes unspoken and so is inaccessible to reevaluation and healing.

Perhaps the best way to learn to help others is to become familiar with the process of self-discovery. It involves learning how to become sensitive to one's own tendencies to error. These can involve patterns of misinterpretation of others' behaviors; limitations of possible responses; false beliefs about oneself, others, the world, or how one should cope with the world; tendencies to bias or distortion regarding certain situations or ideas; unconscious reaction patterns to certain people; and so forth. The student of psychodrama, like any therapist, must become aware of his or her "transferences," those proclivities to react not to who the other person really is, but rather to whose image or memory is evoked by the other person. These distortions must be cleared through the sometimes painful process of personal therapeutic exploration.

Students of psychodrama who are not seeing a psychotherapist to explore their own personal issues should at least participate in an ongoing series of personal growth experiences. The purpose should include not only the correction of personality traits that might interfere with the practice of psychotherapy, but equally importantly, to learn some strategies and develop a motivation to continue one's own self-reflective adventure on a lifelong basis (Schafer, 1982).

Again, take the risk of being the protagonist in your psychodrama training experiences. This not only provides a powerful experience of therapy, but it also helps to sensitize you to the role of the patient in psychodrama. You learn from the inside, so to speak, which of the director's maneuvers are most helpful, and which are most distracting and/or misleading. You identify with and internalize the helpful behaviors, learning through modeling even as you are in the quasi-hypnoidal experience of enactment.

RELATED THERAPEUTIC APPROACHES

Beyond the learning of a basic approach to psychotherapy, which includes the acquisition of an appreciation of the fundamentals of psychodynamic theory, psychosocial development, diagnosis, psychopathology, and at least one mainstream method of treatment, it is also helpful for a student of psychodrama to learn about some therapeutic approaches that are particularly related to psychodrama. Humanistic and existential approaches to psychotherapy share some important viewpoints with Morenean thought and should be included in the development of an overall perspective toward psychology (Seeman, 1982).

Group dynamics is an obvious subject. Moreno considered psychodrama to be most related to group work, although it can also be adapted for use with couples or even individuals (Stein & Callahan, 1982). It is useful for the student of psychodrama to become acquainted with the major literature on group psychotherapy and group dynamics. Moreno's work on sociometry was a related area of concepts and methods that have a good deal of relevance for group work, and the American Board of Examiners requires its candidates to be knowledgeable in this area also.

From the 1950s through the 1970s, group psychotherapy was dominated by the hegemony of psychoanalysis, but gradually, since the mid-1960s, alternative approaches, some of which have been influenced directly or indirectly by Moreno's ideas, have become more recognized. During the 1980s, there have been more interconnections between mainstream group psychotherapy and psychodrama.

A related area is that of *conjoint family therapy*. Interestingly, this approach has always been more active than the traditional analytically oriented forms of group psychotherapy, and though Moreno began with group work, in fact practitioners of family work are often more comfortable with the active nature of directing than those who have been immersed in a more passive approach to individual or group psychotherapy. Another aspect of family therapy that is relevant to students of psychodrama is that its systems orientation offers a more useful framework for the levels of complexity encountered in psychodrama.

Whereas the traditional psychotherapies followed a more mechanistic paradigm that believed a correct diagnosis supposedly led to a precisely aimed intervention, in a more complex system, the number of variables is so great that more general facilitating strategies are required. Moreno's approach to fostering creativity is more congenial to this systems-oriented approach. For example, it is possible for the director to use her awareness of her own ignorance of some of the events in the group as a means for empowering the group: She simply asks someone to double for the group, or for someone who may represent a focus of unclear activity in the group.

Another related modality in psychotherapy is the utilization of the power of *imagery* and *visualization*. This capacity has become recognized as a vehicle for accessing the emotions and reactions of the preverbal psychological functions, sometimes represented by the metaphorical phrase, "the right brain." In the 1970s and 1980s, a variety of approaches to hypnotherapy, especially derived from the work of Milton Erickson, have used this potential of the mind. In developing voluntary control of physiologic functions, using biofeedback as a technical aid, the development of the skill of imagery is a key component. Several other therapeutic approaches specifically use imagery (Assagioli, 1965).

The creative arts therapies also utilize the patients' imagery, and indeed expand their use so that self-expression in aesthetic forms becomes a form of sublimation and empowerment even as it is helping the conscious mind to understand deeper and more subtle dimensions of feeling (Blatner, 1987). Art, music, dance, poetry, and a variety of drama therapy techniques are all potentially powerful sources for expanding the psychodramatist's repertoire. The techniques involved serve as natural vehicles for both the warming-up and working-through processes (Creamer, 1983; McNiff, 1986).

Gestalt therapy was methodologically derived in part from psychodrama, especially regarding the use of the technique of the "empty chair." This rich approach invites an existential and vivid way to access the realm of awareness in the present moment. It is one of the most important complements to the use of psychodrama, and many practitioners freely synthesize both methods.

The *"body therapies"* recognize the importance of the muscular patterns of tension and habitual usage. Bioenergetic Analysis, Alexander Lowen's derivative of Wilhelm Reich's early ideas about character and "body armoring," is perhaps the best known of these approaches (Lowen, 1970). Yet there are elements of this concept in Gestalt therapy and other active treatment methods. Some bioenergetic techniques can be adapted to help patients deal with blocked emotions during psychodramatic explorations.

Working with *nonverbal* communications is an important dimension of psychodrama. In order to bring out the unspoken expressions of emotion, however, the practitioner must first be sensitive to the wide variety of ways that people knowingly or (more often) unknowingly give each other messages (Knapp, 1980; Wainwright, 1980). Related also is a knowledge of patterns of verbal communications, the fields of practical semantics and linguistics that can help the student to understand the common problems of miscommunication that are so prevalent in pathological family interactions (Tannen, 1986).

In addition, the student of psychodrama and psychotherapy should endeavor to reflect on the emerging trends in our culture. Issues related to changing patterns in relations between the sexes, relations with parents and children, the nature of success and philosophies of life, the spiritual journey and religious crises, challenges in educational and vocational choices—these and many other themes are evolving along with new forms of technology and socioeconomic organizations. Political issues relating to ecology, human rights, and the arms race are also factors of increasing relevance to people's lives, and these "sociodramatic" issues often lead to meaningful psychodramas regarding personal values and choices.

The theme of eclecticism is again raised, because, considering these many aspects of life and approaches to therapy, it becomes apparent that the director of psychodrama must be quite flexible to deal with the broad range of problems that present themselves. There are times when enactment is not indicated and more reflective types of therapy would be more helpful. The student must be able to weave in whatever type of help is most appropriate for the situation.

Happily, several approaches to psychotherapy seem to be

emerging with increasing popularity. The cognitive therapies offer a useful balance of psychodynamic orientation without the relatively cost-inefficient disadvantages of the more traditional analytic methods. These therapies have the flexibility to include related modalities such as work with imagery or nonverbal communications, as well as with psychodrama.

In summary, the student of psychodrama must balance several aspects of learning: (1) the knowledge that comes with reading and classroom work; (2) the understanding that comes with experiencing a variety of situations through the exercise of role reversal, as auxiliary, as protagonist, and simply in play; (3) the competence that comes with practice to the point of mastery; and (4) the wisdom that comes from integrating into the learning process one's own personal therapeutic journey, and with it the growing capacity to liberate and access one's own higher self.

REFERENCES

Assagioli, R. (1965). *Psychosynthesis.* New York: Hobbs-Dorman.

Blatner, A. (1987). The function of the creative therapies—a preface. In M. R. Morrison (Ed.), *Poetry as therapy* (pp. 17–19). New York: Human Sciences Press.

Blatner, A. and Blatner, A. (1988). *The art of play: An adult's guide to reclaiming imagination and spontaneity.* New York: Human Sciences Press.

Buchanan, D. R. (1980). The central concern model: A framework for structuring psychodramatic production. *Group Psychotherapy, Psychodrama, & Sociometry, 33,* 47–62.

Creamer, N. (1983). The silent language: Basic principles of movement/dance therapy for the non-movement therapist. *Journal of Group Psychotherapy, Psychodrama & Sociometry, 36*(2), 55–60.

Feder, E. and Feder, B. (1981). *The expressive arts therapies.* Englewood Cliffs, NJ: Prentice-Hall.

Goldman, E. E., Morrison, D. S., and Schramski, T. G. (1982). Co-directing therapy: A method for psychodramatist training. *Journal of Group Psychotherapy, Psychodrama, & Sociometry, 35*(2), 65–69.

Knapp, M. L. (1980). *Essentials of nonverbal communication.* New York: Holt, Rhinehart & Winston.

Lowen, A. (1970). *Pleasure: A creative approach to life.* New York: Coward-McCann.

McNiff, S. (1986). *Educating the creative arts therapist: A profile of the profession.* Springfield, IL: Charles C Thomas.

Nolte, J., and Hale, A. E. (1976). The director's soliloquy and the director's double. *Group Psychotherapy and Psychodrama, 29,* 23–32.

Schafer, R. (1983). *The analytic attitude* (p. 16). New York: Basic Books.

Seeman, H. (1982). A methodology for existential psychotherapy: Psychodrama. *Journal of Group Psychotherapy, Psychodrama & Sociometry, 36*(2), 70–82.

Stein, M. B., and Callahan, M. L. (1982). The use of psychodrama in individual psychotherapy. *Journal of Group Psychotherapy, Psychodrama & Sociometry, 36*(3), 118–129.

Tannen, D. (1986). *That's not what I meant! How conversational style makes or breaks relationships.* New York: Ballantine.

Wainwright, C. J. (1980). A framework for the observation of movements and sounds. *Group Psychotherapy, Psychodrama & Sociometry, 33,* 6–24.

Zuretti, M. (1982). Teaching the psychodramatic method. In M. Pines and L. Rafaelsen (Eds.), *The individual and the group.* New York: Plenum Press.

A Brief History of Psychodrama

The history of psychodrama must begin with the life and work of J. L. Moreno, M.D. His life was eventful and a biography is being prepared by his wife, Zerka and son, Jonathan. I will note some highlights, and a more extensive review is included in my book *Foundations of Psychodrama* (Blatner & Blatner, 1988.)

Jacob Levy Moreno was born on May 19, 1889, in Bucharest, Rumania. In a number of his own earlier books, he gave the date 1892, and also at times said that he was born on a boat in the Black Sea, but this has since been corrected (Bratescu, 1975). He was the oldest of six children, and at the age of five, his family moved to Vienna. Moreno attended the University of Vienna as a student of philosophy and was impressed with the currently popular ideas about creativity such as those presented by Henri Bergson. Around 1908, he also became interested in the play of children in the city's parks, and involved himself as a catalyst, discovering that vitality could be enhanced through encouraging spontaneous forms of dramatics.

Moreno then went on to medical school at the University of Vienna (circa 1912–1917). During this period, he also explored his ideas of a more creative type of theology, developed his philosophy of encounter, and implemented his ideas in social action. For example, he instituted self-help groups for some of the prostitutes in the city; indeed, this may have been one of the first examples of the use of self-help groups and what might today be considered a form of community psychiatry.

Around the end of his medical training Moreno was assigned to be the physician attending a refugee camp in the nearby town of Mittendorf. There he noted patterns of cultural disorganization that might respond to a sociological approach. Bringing to bear his emerging ideas of "encounter" (and he was perhaps the first to use this term), he began to develop his method of sociometry: Assessing the preferences of the people involved in a group, he used this feedback to work out more congenial living arrangements. This may seem obvious today, but at the time it was a highly innovative approach compared with the tendencies of administrators to assign living quarters and jobs on an arbitrary or bureaucratic basis.

In addition, in spite of the stresses of the First World War, and indeed perhaps in part because of them, Vienna was in a ferment of intellectual activity. Moreno plunged into the literary, philosophical, and social milieu of the city. He edited a literary journal, *Daimon,* and included in its contents the writings of such fellow intellectuals as Martin Buber and Max Scheler.

Moreno wrote inspirational poetry and prose. One of his earliest books, *The Words of the Father,* expressed his view that creativity was something that flowed through every individual and that was renewed in every moment (Blatner, 1985). His earliest books were published anonymously, but later, seeing that there was no advantage to this, he had his name attached.

Fascinated by the theater, but feeling that it had become a degraded form, Moreno wanted to see more impromptu acting, more vitality. In many ways, he was anticipating the move toward experimental forms of theater that arose almost a half-century later.

The origin of psychodrama grew out of the convergence of his many interests. The event that might be thought of as the watershed of his ideas was the opening of his "Theatre of Spontaneity" in April, 1921. While this was more an approach to a revitalized theater for the people rather than a form of psychotherapy, it soon became apparent that for the actors it was indeed a healing experience. His "Stegreif-theatre" involved a group of actors (including the later famous Peter Lorre) who at first performed what were some of the first forms of improvisational dramas, focused on events of the day: "The Living Newspaper." Later on, in smaller groups, Moreno used the method to deal more with personal and interpersonal problems. The book on the subject, *The Theatre of Spontaneity*, that he wrote in 1923 presented perhaps the first proposal for a "theatre in the round." During this time, he lived in the Viennese suburb of Voslau and served the community as their public health officer and family physician.

Because postwar Vienna was poor, disorganized, and unable to sustain his experimental efforts, Moreno decided to emigrate to the United States. (He thought of going to the new experiment of socialist Russia, but decided he needed a far greater degree of freedom.) Arriving in New York in 1925, he was able to introduce his ideas to the various hospitals and clinics in the area.

Moreno was a man of many talents. He had invented something like a wire recorder, and it was with the sponsorship of a businessman in the United States that he was able to immigrate. Later on, he wrote some of the earliest papers about the possible applications of both audio and video recording in psychotherapy.

In the 1930s, Moreno consulted with prisons, residential treatment centers for delinquent and retarded adolescents, and various other facilities. These experiences fitted with his orientation as a psychiatrist dedicated to social concerns. He coined the term "group psychotherapy" in 1932, and became one of the pioneers of the emergence of this method. He continued to develop his theoretical and practical ideas about sociometry, and in 1934 published *Who Shall Survive? A New Approach to the Problem of Human Interrelations*. This weighty book included many of his early ideas about psychodrama, role theory, and social psychology. Sociometry went on to become a significant method in sociology, especially around the mid-1950s, and the journal *Sociometry: A Journal of Interpersonal Relations*, which he initiated, is still published by the American Sociological Society.

In 1936, Moreno opened a sanitarium in Beacon, New York, about 60 miles north of New York City on the Hudson River. He built a theater designed specifically for psychodrama and began to treat patients using that method. This became his home and the hub of a number of related activities. He published his own professional monographs and journals.

Moreno had contacts with a number of other pioneers and thought he had been influential in the development of their work: S. R. Slavson in 1931; Alfred Korzybski (who originated the field of semantics) in 1935; Kurt Lewin in 1936; and a number of his students in the subsequent years. For these reasons, Moreno felt that he deserved more credit in the ensuing years, especially regarding the origins of the ideas that gave rise to the "T-Group," sensitivity training, and the encounter group movement (Bradford et al., 1964).

During the Second World War, Moreno continued to practice, opened an institute for training in New York City, did sociometric studies in schools in the area, and organized the first professional association devoted to group psychotherapy, which evolved into the American Society of Group Psychotherapy and Psychodrama (ASGPP). After the war, Moreno began to publish other journals, more mono-graphs, books, and articles. At the beginning of the 1940s, he met Zerka Toeman, who became professionally associated with him (Moreno, 1970). They were married in 1949, and together they began to teach and present Moreno's ideas and methods throughout the United States and internationally.

Moreno's work served as one of the major alternatives to the nondirective and analytic methods from the 1940s through the early 1960s. In this role, Moreno actively encour-aged a wide range of other forms of psychotherapy. He used his journals and the professional meetings of the ASGPP as vehicles for the promotion of such approaches as dance therapy, poetry therapy, family therapy, and so forth. Psy-chodramatic methods have since been integrated into many of the "innovative" approaches that have emerged since the 1960s, such as "family sculpture" (another name for "action sociometry"), Gestalt therapy, and so on. In addition, psy-chodramatic elements are used in conjunction with Adlerian therapy and behavior therapy, among others.*

Moreno collaborated with a number of leaders in the field

---

*Eric Berne wrote: "In his selection of specific techniques, Dr. Perls shares with other 'active' psychotherapists the 'Moreno problem': The fact that nearly all known 'active' techniques were first tried out by Dr. J. L. Moreno in psychodrama, so that it is difficult to come up with an original idea in this regard." From a review of Gestalt Therapy Verbatim, *American Journal of Psychiatry*, 126(10: 15–20,), April 1970.

A. H. Maslow (the "dean" of American humanistic psychology) wrote, regarding Jane Howard's article on Esalen and other new developments in education and psychotherapy, "I would however like to add one credit-where-credit-is-due foot-note. Many of the techniques set forth in the article were originally invented by Dr. Jacob Moreno, who is still functioning vigorously and probably still inventing new techniques and ideas." (Letter to Editors, LIFE Magazine, August 2, 1968).

Dr. William Schutz (a major figure in the American encounter group movement) noted that ". . . Virtually all of the methods that I had proudly compiled or invented [Moreno] had more or less anticipated, in some cases forty years earlier . . .," "Leuner's original article (on guided fantasy) has appeared in (Moreno's) Journal in about 1932, and he had been using the method periodically since . . . I invite you to investigate Moreno's work. It is probably not sufficiently acknowledged in this country. Perl's Gestalt Therapy owes a great deal to it. It is imaginative and worth exploring." (*Here Comes Everybody*, Harper & Row, 1971.)

of mental health. He and Zerka were major organizers of the first international conferences of group psychotherapy, along with S. H. Foulkes of Great Britain, S. Lebovici of France, and other eminent figures. Beginning with a group called the International Committee of Group Psychotherapy, the attendees began planning in Paris in 1951, and held its first meeting in Toronto in 1954. The Second International Congress was held in Zurich in 1957; the Third in Milan in 1963; the Fourth in Vienna in 1968; and the Fifth was in Zurich in 1973. At that time, the name of the group was changed to the International Association of Group Psychotherapy. These conferences were usually attended by over 1,000 participants each time.

Meanwhile, Moreno also began to organize a series of International Congresses of Psychodrama and Sociodrama: First, Paris, 1964; Second, Barcelona, 1966; Third, Prague, 1968; Fourth, Buenos Aires, 1969; Fifth, Sao Paulo, Brazil, 1970; Sixth, Amsterdam, 1971; and Seventh, Tokyo, 1972. These demonstrated the widespread reception of psychodrama, and Moreno's books were translated into many languages, along with books on psychodrama being produced by many writers in these other countries.

Moreno's energy, vitality, charisma, and drive were remarkable. He had his faults, too: Like a number of other innovators, he was often insensitive to group and personal politics. Yet the sheer range of interests and the validity of his vision combine to generate a powerful complex of ideas that continue to find increasing appreciation as relevant to the challenges of today's world.

In May 1974, after a period of gradual decline of his health, Moreno decided to die and stopped eating. He received visitors who came to pay their respects and died soon after the annual meeting of the ASGPP. Since that time, Zerka Moreno has continued to carry on the work, teaching all over the world, writing, and encouraging others. She also fostered more democratic participation and control in the ASGPP.

The international conferences continue under the leadership of The International Association of Group Psychotherapy. Its meetings address a wide variety of subjects and include a regular component of presentations that deal with psychodrama. After Moreno's death, and yet continuing to maintain Moreno's name on its letterhead as the founder, the Congresses have been held as follows: Sixth, Philadelphia, 1977; Seventh, Copenhagen, 1980; Eighth, Mexico City, 1984; Ninth, Zagreb (Yugoslavia), 1986; and the Tenth, Amsterdam, 1989. International meetings of psychodrama continue also in such locations as Argentina, Australia, Italy, and Japan.

In summary, the field of psychodrama continues to emerge as a source of ideas for a more integrative approach to psychotherapy. It addresses and includes themes that are increasingly relevant in a time of change. Some of the philosophical ideas that were rather incongruent with the intellectual ambience of the mid-twentieth century are now becoming more relevant and acceptable. Transpersonal psychology continues to influence a growing number of professionals. Yet Moreno's contribution suggests that there are also transpersonal elements in the development of approaches to fostering creativity, compassion, and a capacity to more effectively build toward the future. I shall end with a review of some of the major themes that Moreno introduced into the field (Table 2).

TABLE 2 Some of the Themes and Concepts that Moreno Emphasized in His Writings

1. Play as an element in culture and the helping relationship.
2. Catharsis—its place in history, drama, religion, and psychodrama.
3. The place of warm-up in everyday life—e.g., boxing, sexual activity, group process, psychotherapy.
4. Imagination—the creative potential; applications of fantasy.

TABLE 2 *(continued)*

5. Spontaneity and creativity as primary elements of human growth.
6. The importance of nonverbal communication, body tone and move-ment, posture, position, territoriality, lighting, sound, music, col-ors, textures, body contact, laughter, and humor as elements in human relationships.
7. The social network, family network, community and societal network, and *interpersonal transaction* (therapeutic milieu).
8. Here-and-now—an essentially existential approach.
9. Focus on *process* rather than *content*.
10. Acting-out (in the service of the ego) as an expression of act hunger, possibility as a synthetic rather than dissociative phenomenon.
11. The religious implications and applications of subjective, creative, and spontaneous human beings in relation to a creative cosmos.
12. Utilization of a wide variety of methods, techniques, and technologies to help clients explore dimensions of their experience (rather than restriction to one technique), i.e., eclecticism.
13. The applications of role reversal to childrearing, the teaching of empathy and interpersonal sensitivity.
14. The use of therapy *in situ* (i.e., the intervention on-the-spot, exploring the problem in the context and social network from which it arose), now applied in milieu therapy, residential treatment centers for children ' adolescents, and other contexts.

REFERENCES

Blatner, A. (Fall, 1985). Moreno's "process philosophy." *Journal of Group Psychotherapy, Psychodrama & Sociometry, 38*(3), 133–136.

Blatner, A. (1988). *Foundations of psychodrama: History, theory, and practice.* New York: Springer Publishing Co.

Bradford, L., Gibb, J. R., and Benne, K. D. (1964). *T-Group theory and laboratory method: Innovations in re-education.* New York: John Wiley.

Bratescu, G. (1975). The date and birthplace of J. L. Moreno. *Group Psychotherapy, Psychodrama & Sociometry, 28*, 2–4.

Buchanan, D. R. (1981). Forty-one years of psychodrama at St. Elizabeths Hospital. *Journal of Group Psychotherapy, Psychodrama & Sociometry, 34*, 134–147.

Corsini, R. J. (1955). Historic background of group psychotherapy. *Group Psychotherapy, 8*(3), 219–225.

Fox, J. (1978). Moreno and his theatre. *Group Psychotherapy, Psychodrama, & Sociometry, 31,* 109–116.

Gazda, G. (Ed.). (1968). *Innovations in group psychotherapy.* Springfield, IL: Charles C Thomas.

Hare, A. P. (Fall, 1986). Moreno's contribution to social psychology. *Journal of Group Psychotherapy, Psychodrama, & Sociometry, 39*(3), 85–94.

Kraus, C., and Clouse, J. (Spring, 1986). Report from the J. L. Moreno collection. *Journal of Group Psychotherapy, Psychodrama, & Sociometry, 39*(1), 41–44. (Collection in the rare books and manuscripts department, F. A. Countway Library of Medicine in Boston.)

Leutz, G. A. (1978). Recent developments of psychodrama in Western Europe. *Group Psychotherapy, Psychodrama, & Sociometry, 31,* 168–173.

Meiers, J. (1949). Origins and development of group psychotherapy: Historical survey, 1930–1945. *Sociometry, 8*(4), 499–530.

Moreno, J. L. (1969). The Viennese origins of the encounter movement. *Group Psychotherapy, 22*(3–4), 7–16.

Moreno, J. L. (1970). Is God a single person? My first encounter with a muse of high order, Zerka. *Group Psychotherapy, 23*(3–4), 75–78.

Moreno, Z. T. (1967). The seminal mind of J. L. Moreno and his influence upon the present generation. *Group Psychotherapy, 20*(3–4), 218–229.

Moreno, Z. T. (1976). In memoriam: Jacob L(evy) Moreno. *Group Psychotherapy, Psychodrama & Sociometry, 29,* 130–135.

Renouvier, P. (1955). The group psychotherapy movement and J. L. Moreno. *Group Psychotherapy, 11*(1–2), 69–88.

Sacks, J. M. (1977). Reminiscence of J. L. Moreno. *Group, 1*(3), 194–200.

Treadwell, T., and Treadwell, J. (1972). The pioneer of the group encounter movement. *Group Psychotherapy, 25*(1–2), 16–26.

Weiner, H. B. (1968). J. L. Moreno—Mr. Group Psychotherapy. *Group Psychotherapy, 21*(3–4), 144–150.

Whitaker, C. (1988). Foreword. In. J. Fox (Ed.), *The essential Moreno.* New York: Springer Publishing Co.

Yablonsky, L. (1975). Psychodrama lives. *Human Behavior, 4,* 25–29.

Bibliography

This bibliography is designed to aid the reader in finding some of the most relevant materials currently available. This is not an exhaustive listing of writings in the field, and many other references on psychodrama may be found in the various books by Blatner, Corsini, Gendron, Greer, and Kipper. In addition, the books by Ancelin-Schutzenberger, Leutz, and Petzold have extensive references to other items in the professional literature in Europe and other countries. References that are more related to specific subjects are noted in the sections following each chapter in this book. (Especially note those regarding applications in various fields at the end of Chapter 8.)

JOURNALS

It may help to know that most of the articles in the psychodrama literature are to be found in the journals that Moreno founded. Some of these have changed their name several times.

Sociometry: A Journal of Interpersonal Relations, Vols. 1–18, 1937–1956. The early volumes contain some of Moreno's basic ideas and reflect their eclectic format through the wide variety of people who were published in them. In 1956, this journal was turned over to the American Sociological Society.

International Journal of Sociometry, Vols. 1–5, 1956–1968.

Handbook of International Sociometry, Vols. 6–8, 1971–1973.

Sociatry (subtitled A Journal of Group and Intergroup Therapy), Vols. 1–3, 1947–1950. Then, title changed to:
Group Psychotherapy, Vols. 4–22, 1951–1970. Then . . .
Group Psychotherapy and Psychodrama, Vols. 23–28, 1970–1975. The journal continued following Moreno's death in 1974, edited by a committee of leaders in the field of psychodrama, titled:
Group Psychotherapy, Psychodrama, and Sociometry, Vols. 29–33, 1976–1980. Many of the back issues of these journals (before 1981) may be obtained by writing to Beacon House, Inc., Welsh Road and Butler Pike, Ambler, PA 19002. Since that time, the journal, under the editorship of the American Society for Group Psychotherapy and Psychodrama, has been titled:
Journal of Group Psychotherapy, Psychodrama, & Sociometry, Vols. 34+, 1981 through the present. (Published by Heldref Publications, 4000 Albermarle Street, N.W., Washington, DC 20016.)

GENERAL BIBLIOGRAPHY

Anzieu, D. (1979). *Le psychodrame analytique de l'enfant et de l'adolescent* (2nd ed.). Paris: P. U. F. French.

Bentley, E. (1977). Theatre and therapy. In W. Anderson (Ed.), *Therapy and the arts* (pp. 29–50). New York: Harper/Colophon.

Bischof, L. J. (1964). *Interpreting personality theories* (pp. 355–420). New York: Harper & Row.

Blatner, H. A. (Ed.) (1968). *Practical aspects of psychodrama*. Belmont, CA: Author. (Out of print.)

Blatner, H. A. (Ed.) (1970). *Psychodrama, role-playing and action methods: Theory and practice*. Thetford, England: Author. (This was a revision and expansion of the previous book, also now out of print.)

Blatner, H. A. (Later, his name changed to H. Adam Blatner and then Adam Blatner.) (1973). *Acting-In: Practical applications of psychodramatic methods* (1st ed.). New York: Springer Publishing Co.

Blatner, A. (1985). *Creating your living: Applications of psychodramatic methods in everyday life*. San Marcos, TX: Author. (Out of print.)

Blatner, A. (1988). Psychodrama. In R. J. Corsini and D. Wedding (Eds.), *Current Psychotherapies* (4th ed.). Itasca, IL: F. E. Peacock.

Blatner, A. (In preparation). *Role dynamics: An integrative psychosocial theory*.

Blatner, A. and Blatner, A. (1988). *The art of play: An adult's guide to reclaiming imagination and spontaneity.* New York: Human Sciences Press.

Blatner, A. and Blatner, A. (1988). *Foundations of psychodrama: History, theory, and practice.* New York: Springer Publishing Co.

Blatner, A. and Blatner, A. (1988). The metaphysics of creativity as reflected in Moreno's "metapraxie" and the mystical tradition. *Journal of Group Psychotherapy, Psychodrama & Sociometry, 40*(4), 155–163.

Boal, A. (1985). *Theatre of the oppressed.* New York: Theatre Communications Group. (Applications of Morenean-like ideas and methods in Latin America.)

Boies, K. G. (1973). Role playing as a behavior change technique: Review of the empirical literature. In Isaac M. Marks et. al. (Eds.), *Psychotherapy and behavior change, 1972.* Chicago: Aldine.

Borgatta, E. F., Boguslaw, R., and Haskell, M. (1975). On the work of Jacob L. Moreno. *Sociometry, 38*(1), 148–161.

Boria, G. (1983). *Tele: Manuale di psicodramma classico.* Milano: Franco Angeli.

Bouquet, C. M. (1982). Theory of the scene. In M. Pines and L. Rafaelsen (Eds.), *The individual and the group* (pp. 179–186). New York: Plenum Press.

Buchanan, D. R. (1984). Moreno's social atom: A diagnostic and treatment tool for exploring interpersonal relationships. *The Arts in Psychotherapy, 11,* 155–164

Buchanan, D. R. (1984). Chapter 18: Psychodrama. In Tokasz B. Karasu (Ed.), *The psychiatric therapies, Part 2: the psychosocial therapies.* Washington, D.C.: The American Psychiatric Association. (This is an excellent brief summary of the subject!)

Buchanan, D. R., and Taylor, J. A. (1986). Jungian typology of professional psychodramatists: Myers-Briggs type indicator analysis of certified psychodramatists. *Psychological Reports, 58,* 391–400.

Bulletin de psychologie (1969–70). Vol. 285, No. 13–16. Ed. by Université de Paris. (Special edition on psychodrama.)

Burwell, D. M. (1969). Psychodrama. *Canadian Journal of Occupational Therapists, 36,* 141–144.

Bustos, D. (1974). *Psicoterapia psicodramatica.* Buenos Aires: Paidos.

Carp, E. A. (1949). *Psychodrama.* Amsterdam: Scheltema & Holkema.

Cohen, R. G., and Lipkin, G. B. (1979). Psychodrama. In *Therapeutic group work for health professionals* (pp. 179–217). New York: Springer Publishing Co.

Corsini, R. J. (1968). Immediate therapy in groups. In G. M. Gazda (Ed.), *Innovations to group psychotherapy.* Springfield, IL: Charles C Thomas.

Corsini, R. J., and Putzey, L. J. (1956). The historic background of group psychotherapy. *Group Psychotherapy*, 9, 177–249. (A 1700-item bibliography including items dating from 1906–1955.)

Corsini, R. J. (1967). *Role playing in psychotherapy.* Chicago, IL: Aldine. (Very good, with annotated bibliography.)

Corsini, R. J. (1973). The behind-the-back encounter. In L. R. Wolberg and E. K. Schwartz (Eds.), *Group therapy, 1973.* New York: Intercontinental Medical Book Corp.

Emunah, R. (1983). Drama therapy with adult psychiatric patients. *The Arts In Psychotherapy*, 10, 77–84.

Fine, Leon J. (1978). Psychodrama. In Raymond I. Corsini (Ed.), *Current psychotherapies* (2nd ed.). Itasca, IL: F. E. Peacock.

Fleshman, B., and Fryrear, J. (1981). *The arts in therapy.* Chicago: Nelson-Hall. (Excellent review of the various Expressive Therapies.)

Fox, J. (Ed.). (1987). *The essential Moreno: Writings on psychodrama, group method, and spontaneity.* New York: Springer Publishing Co. (A collection of articles by J. L. Moreno.)

Gendron, J. (1980). *Moreno: The roots and the branches; and bibliography of psychodrama, 1972–1980.* Beacon, N.Y.: Beacon House. (Good source of references.)

Goldman, E. E., and Morrison, D. S. (1984). *Psychodrama: Experience and process.* Phoenix, AZ: Eldemar Corp. (5812 N. 12th St. #32, Phoenix, Ariz. 85014)

Greenberg, I. A. (1968). *Psychodrama and audience attitude change.* Beverly Hills: Behavioral Studies Press.

Greenberg, I. A. (Ed.). (1974). *Psychodrama: Theory and therapy.* New York: Behavioral Publications.

Greenberg, I. A. (Ed.). (1977). *Group hypnotherapy and hypnodrama* (pp. 231–303). Chicago: Nelson-Hall.

Greenberg, I. A. (1986). Psychodrama. In I. L. Kutash and A. Wolf (Eds.), *Psychotherapist's casebook.* San Francisco: Jossey-Bass.

Greer, V. J. and Sacks, J. M. (1973). *Bibliography of psychodrama (1920–1972).* Authors. (834 items.)

Gregoric, L., and Gregoric, M. (1981). Sociodrama: Video in social action. In J. L. Fryrear & B. Fleshman (Eds.), *Videotherapy in mental health.* Springfield, IL: Charles C Thomas.

Haas, R. B. (1949). *Psychodrama and sociodrama in American education.* Beacon, NY: Beacon House.

Haas, R. B., and Moreno, J. L. (1961). Psychodrama as a projective technique. In H. H. Anderson and G. L. Anderson (Eds.) *An introduction to projective techniques.* Englewood Cliffs, NJ: Prentice-Hall.

Hale, A. E. (1981). *Conducting clinical sociometric explorations: A manual for psychodramatists and sociometrists.* Roanoke, VA: Royal Publishing. (This is the best introduction to the method.)

Hare, A. P. (1985). *Social interaction as drama.* Beverly Hills, CA: Sage Publications.

Hare, A. P. (1986). Bibliography of the work of J. L. Moreno. *Journal of Group Psychotherapy, Psychodrama, and Sociometry, 39*(3), 95–128.

Haskell, M. R. (1975). *Socioanalysis: Self direction via sociometry and psychodrama.* Long Beach: Role Training Assoc.

Haskell, R. J., Pearl, C. E., and Haskell, M. R. (1986). *A world in microcosm: Psychodrama and related subjects.* (Previously titled *Sociometry through group interaction psychotherapy.* Long Beach, CA: Role Training Associates (1750 E. Ocean Blvd., Long Beach, CA 90802).

Heilveil, I. (1983). *Video in mental health practice* (pp. 60–67). New York: Springer Publishing Co.

Heisey, M. J. (1982). *Clinical case studies in psychodrama.* Washington, D.C.: University Press of America.

Hollander, C. E. (1973). Role playing: An action learning process. *Handbook of International Sociometry, 8,* 88–93.

Hollander, C. E. (1978). Psychodrama, role playing and sociometry: Living and learning processes. In D. Kurpius (Ed.), *Learning: Making learning environments more effective* (pp. 168–241). Muncie, IN: Accelerated Development, Inc.

Hollander, C. E. (1978). *A process for psychodrama training: The Hollander psychodrama curve* (revised ed.). Denver: Snow Lion Press.

Hudgins, M. K., and Kiesler, D. J. (1984). *Instructional manual for doubling in individual psychotherapy.* Richmond, VA: Author.

Irwin, E. C., and Portner, E. (Eds.) (1984). *The scope of drama therapy: Proceedings from the first annual drama therapy conference.* New Haven, CT: N. A. D. T.

Jennings, S. (1974). *Remedial drama.* New York: Theatre Arts Books.

Jennings, S. (1986). *Creative drama in group work.* London: Winslow Press. (Many useful techniques.)

Kipper, D. A. (1986). *Psychotherapy through clinical role playing.* New York: Brunner/Mazel. (Excellent and thorough text.)

Klein, A. F. (1956). *Role playing in leadership training and group problem solving.* New York: Association Press.

Krojanker, R. (1963). Some new techniques in psychodrama and hypnodrama. *Archives de Criminologia, Neuro-Psiquiatria (Quito), 11,* 411–432.

Kumar, V. K., and Treadwell, T. W. (1985). *Practical sociometry for psychodramatists.* West Chester, PA: Authors.

Landy, R. J. (1986). *Drama therapy: Concepts and Practices*. Springfield, IL: Charles C Thomas.

Lebovici, S. (1974). A combination of psychodrama and psycho-analysis. In Stefan de Schill (Ed.), *The challenge for group psychotherapy: Present and future* (pp. 286–315). New York: International Universities Press.

Lee, R. H. (1981). Video as adjunct to psychodrama and role playing. In J. L. Fryrear and B. Fleshman (Eds.), *Videotherapy in mental health*. Springfield, IL: Charles C Thomas.

Lemoine, G., and Lemoine, P. (1972). *Le psychodrame*. Paris: Laffont.

Leutz, G. A. (1971). Transference, empathy, and tele. *Group Psychotherapy & Psychodrama*, 24(3–4), 107–112.

Leutz, G. A. (1974). *Psychodrama: Theory and practice*. Berlin: Springer-Verlag. (In German.)

Leutz, G. A., and Petzold, H. (Eds.). (1970). *Zeistchrift fur praktische psychologie*, 5(8). (Special issue on psychodrama, in German.)

Leutz, G. A., and Oberborbeck, K. (Eds.). (1980). Psychodrama. *Gruppenpsychotherapie und Gruppendynamik*, 19(3–4). (Entire issue, in German.)

Leveton, E. (1977). *Psychodrama for the timid clinician*. New York; Springer.

Luchins, A. S. (1964). Role playing and psychodrama. In *Group therapy: A guide* (pp. 48–59). New York: Random House.

Matsumura, K. (1986). Spontaneity. *The Journal of the Science of Relationships*, 14(1), 30–40. Tokyo, Japan.

McReynolds, P., and DeVoge, S. (1977). Use of improvisational techniques in assessment. In P. McReynolds (Ed.), *Advances in psychological assessment* (Vol. 4). San Francisco: Jossey-Bass.

Menegazzo, C. M. (1981). *Magia, mito, y psicodrama* (Spanish). Buenos Aires: Editorial Paidos.

Miller, M. M. (1971). *Psychodrama: The self on stage*. Washington, DC: The New School of Psychotherapy.

Moreno, J. J. (1980). Musical psychodrama: A new direction in music therapy. *Journal of Music Therapy*, 17(1), 34–42. (The author is J. L. Moreno's nephew, a noted music therapist.)

Moreno, J. L. Note: The originator of psychodrama was a prolific writer, publishing scores of articles and monographs on the subject, only a few of which we need mention here. A complete listing of his works has been noted by Hare (1986) (q.v.). Moreno also wrote scores of articles on group psychotherapy and sociometry. His books and articles have been translated into many languages. You will notice that most of his books were published by Beacon House, which was Moreno's own publishing house, named in honor of his home and sanitarium in Beacon, New York. Until his death, he also supervised the publication of the major journals devoted to psychodrama, sociometry, and group psychotherapy. Following Moreno's death, the sales of his remaining books were taken over by the Horsham Clinic, and may be obtained by writing to Beacon House, Inc., Welsh Road and Butler Pike, Ambler, PA 19002. Some of his better known and more substantial writings are listed here.

Moreno, J. L. (1921). *The Words of the Father*, first published anonymously in Vienna; inspirational poetry and some exposition of Moreno's philosophical-theological ideas. (Also entitled *The psychodrama of God: A new hypothesis of the self.*) Re-issued in 1971. Beacon, NY: Beacon House.

Moreno, J. L. (1923). *The theater of spontaneity.* (First published in Potsdam with the title, *Das Stegreiftheatre,* and translated and published by Beacon House in 1947 and 1972.)

Moreno, J. L. (1934). *Who shall survive? A new approach to the problem of human interrelations.* Washington, DC: Nervous & Mental Disease Publishing Co. (In 1953, this was revised and expanded, and the subtitle changed to become: *Who shall survive? Foundations of sociometry, group psychotherapy, and sociodrama.* Beacon, NY: Beacon House.)

Moreno, J. L. (1946). *Psychodrama* (Vol. 1). (Republished, 1972.) Beacon, NY: Beacon House.

Moreno, J. L. (Ed.) (1946). *Group Psychotherapy: A symposium.* Beacon, NY: Beacon House.

Moreno, J. L. (1951). (Ed.) *Sociometry: Experimental method and the science of society.* Beacon, NY: Beacon House.

Moreno, J. L. (1956). *Sociometry and the science of man.* Beacon, NY: Beacon House.

Moreno, J. L. (Ed.). (1956–1960). *Progress in psychotherapy* (Vols. 1–5), coedited with Frieda Fromm-Reichmann (Vol. 1), and then Jules Masserman (Vols. 2–5), both of whom were the first names on the books. New York: Grune & Stratton. (This series of five books contains a number of important articles on psychodrama by Moreno and others.)

Moreno, J. L. (1960). *The sociometry reader,* co-edited with Helen Hall Jennings and others. Glencoe, IL: The Free Press.

Moreno, J. L. (1963). Reflections on my method of group psychotherapy and psychodrama. *CIBA Symposium,* 2(4), 148–157. (Reprinted in 1974 in H. Greenwald (Ed.), *Active Psychotherapy.* New York: Jason Aronson.)

Moreno, J. L. (1969). *Psychodrama, Vol. 3.* Beacon, NY: Beacon House.

Moreno, J. L. (1971). Psychodrama. In H. I. Kaplan & B. Sadock (Eds.), *Comprehensive group psychotherapy*. Baltimore, MD: Williams & Wilkins.

Moreno, J. L. (1972). The religion of God–Father. In Paul E. Johnson (Ed.), *Healer of the mind: A psychiatrist's search for faith*. Nashville, TN: Abington.

Moreno, J. L. (1987). *The essential Moreno*. (Edited by Jonathan Fox: see reference under that name.) New York: Springer.

Moreno, J. L., and Elefthery, D. G. (1975). An introduction to group psychodrama. In George Gazda (Ed.), *Basic approaches to group psychotherapy and group counseling* (2nd. Ed.). Springfield, IL: Charles C Thomas.

Moreno, J. L., Friedemann, A., Battegay, R., and Moreno, Z. (Eds.). (1966). *International handbook of group psychotherapy*. New York: Philosophical Library.

Moreno, J. L., and Moreno, Z. T. (1959). *Psychodrama, Vol. 2*. Beacon, NY: Beacon House.

Moreno, J. L., and Zeleny, L. D. (1958). Role theory and Sociodrama. In J. S. Roucek, *Contemporary Sociology*. New York: Philosophical Library.

Moreno, Z. T. (1951). Psychodrama in a well baby clinic. *Group Psychotherapy, 4*(1–2), 100–106.

Moreno, Z. T. (1959). A survey of psychodramatic techniques. *Group Psychotherapy, 12*, 5–14.

Moreno, Z. T. (1965). Psychodramatic rules, techniques, and adjunctive methods. *Group Psychotherapy, 18*(1–2), 73–86.

Moreno, Z. T. (1983). Psychodrama. In H. I. Kaplan & B. J. Sadock (Eds.), *Comprehensive group psychotherapy* (2nd ed.). Baltimore: Williams & Wilkins.

Moreno, Z. T. (1987). Psychodrama. In Jeffrey Zeig (Ed.), *The evolution of psychotherapy*. New York: Brunner/Mazel.

Murray, N. (1976). Psychodrama—post Moreno. In A. Wolberg & M. Aronson (Eds.), *Group therapy, 1976—An overview* (pp. 16–20). New York: Stratton Intercontinental Medical Book Corp.

O'Connell, W. E. (1975). *Action therapy and Adlerian theory*. Chicago: Alfred Adler Institute.

O'Connell, W. E. (1978). Action therapy. *Individual Psychologist, 15*(3), 4–11.

Ohlsen, M. M. (1969). Role Playing. In *Group counseling*. New York: Holt, Rinehart & Winston.

Olsson, P. A. (1980). Psychodrama and literature in evaluation and treatment. In H. S. Moffic and G. L. Adams (Eds.), *A clinician's manual on mental health care: A multidisciplinary approach* (pp. 130–138). Menlo Park, CA: Addison–Wesley.

Olsson, P. A., and Barth, P. A. (1983). New uses of Psychodrama. *Journal of Operational Psychiatry, 14*(2), 95–101.

Pavlovsy, E., et al. (1979). *Psicodrama cuando y por que dramatizar.* Madrid: Fundamentos.

Petzold, H., and Mathias, U. (1982). *Rollenentwicklung und Identitat.* (Role Development and Identity—German) Paderborn, Junfermann.

Petzold, H. (Ed.). (1985). *Dramatische therapie.* (German) Stuttgart: Hippokrates Verlag. (Contains many references of articles in German, French.)

Polansky, N. A. (1982). Chapter 11: Ego functions in psychodrama. In *Integrated ego psychology.* New York: Aldine.

Portner, E. (Ed.). (1986). *Drama therapy in print: A bibliography.* (38 pages.) New Haven, CT: N. A. D. T.

Rabson, J. S. (1979). *Psychodrama: Theory and method.* Cape Town (South Africa): University of Cape Town Department of Sociology. (Now out of print).

Sacks, J. M. (1974). The psychodramatic approach. In Donald S. Milman and George D. Goldman, (Eds.) *Group process today: Evaluation and perspectives.* Springfield, IL: Charles C Thomas.

Sacks, J. M. (1981). Drama therapy with the acting out patient. In G. Schattner & R. Courtney (Eds.), *Drama in therapy* (Vol. 2—Adults) (pp. 35–56). New York: Drama Book Specialists.

Schattner, G. & Courtney, R. (Eds.) (1981). *Drama in therapy* (Vol. 1— Children; Vol. II—Adults). New York: Drama Book Specialists. (Excellent anthology with many relevant articles.)

Schramski, T. (1982). *A systematic model of psychodrama.* Tucson, AZ: Author.

Schumacher-Merz, I. (1982). Dependence-independence-interdependence of the individual within the group: Possibilities of diagnosis and intervention by means of psychodrama. In M. Pines & L. Rafaelsen (Eds.), *The individual and the group* (pp. 173–178). New York: Plenum Press.

Seabourne, B. (1985). *Practical aspects of psychodrama.* St Louis: Author. [Papers first privately produced in 1966 and included in Blatner's 1968 and 1970 books (q.v.). May be obtained by writing to author at 546 Oakwood, St. Louis, 63119.]

Schutzenberger, A. (1970). *Précis de psychodrama* (revised ed.). Paris: Editions Universitaires.

Schutzenberger, A. (1975). *Introduction to role playing: Sociodrama, psychodrama, and their application to social work, everyday life, education and psychotherapy.* Toulouse, France: Edouard Privat. (In French.)

Schutzenberger, A., & Weil, P. (1977). *Psicodrama triadico.* Belo Horizonte, Brazil: Interlivros.

Siroka, R. W., Siroka, E., & Schloss, G. (Eds.) (1971). *Sensitivity training and group encounter—An introduction.* New York: Grosset & Dunlap. (Section on psychodrama.)

Siroka, R. W. (1978). From drama to psychodrama. *Art Psychotherapy, 5,* 15–17.

Starr, A. (1977). *Psychodrama: Rehearsal for living.* Chicago: Nelson-Hall.

Swink, D. F., & Buchanan, D. R. (1984). The effects of sociodramatic goal-oriented role play and non-goal oriented role play on locus of control. *Journal of Clinical Psychology, 40*(5), 1178–1183.

Torrance, E. P. (1978). Sociodrama and the creative process (#14). In Frederic Flach (Ed.), *Creative Psychiatry.* Geigy Pharmaceuticals.

Torrance, E. P., Murdock, M., & Fletcher, D. (In press). *Sociodrama: Creative problem solving in action.* Buffalo, NY: Bearly Limited.

Treadwell, T. W. (Ed.). (1974). *Confrontation and training via the group process—The action techniques.* New York: Simon & Schuster (Selected Academic Readings).

Vander May, J. H. (1981). *Psychodrama á deux.* Monograph available from author at Pine Rest Christian Hospital, 300 68th St. So., Grand Rapids, MI 49508.

Warner, G. D. (1978–1986). *Psychodrama training tips* (Vols. 1 & 2). 326 Summit Ave, Hagerstown, Maryland, 21740.

Weil, P. (1967). *Psicodrama.* Rio de Janeiro: Edicons Cepa. (In Portuguese).

Weiner, H. B. (1967). The identity of the psychodramatist and the underground of psychodrama. *Group Psychotherapy, 20*(3–4), 114–117.

Weiner, H. B. (1975). Living experiences with death—A journeyman's view through psychodrama. *Omega, 6*(3), 251–274. (Variety of techniques.)

Weiner, H. B. (1981). Return from splendid isolation. In G. Schattner & R. Courtney (Eds.), *Drama in therapy* (pp. 129–156). New York: Drama Book Specialists.

Wolberg, A. R. (1976). The contributions of Jacob Moreno. In Lewis R. Wolbert & M. L. Aronson (Eds.), *Group therapy, 1976—An overview.* New York: Stratton Intercontinental Medical Book Corp. (There are some other fine articles that are also relevant in this book.)

Yablonsky, L. (1972). Psychodrama and role training. In L. N. Solomon & B. Berzon (Eds.). *New perspectives on encounter groups.* San Francisco: Jossey-Bass.

Yablonsky, L. (1975). *Psychodrama: Resolving emotional problems through role-playing.* New York: Basic Books.

Index